D0807878

BEGINNING ON BOUNDARY

An Orphan's Story

Rosemary Capanna

Beginning on Boundary
An Orphan's Story

© 2018 Rosemary Capanna
All Rights Reserved

BeginningonBoundary.com

The website addresses used in this book
are offered as a resource to readers.
This is not meant to imply endorsement.

This is a creative telling of my mom's true story.
Some situations and dialogue have been imagined,
and a few names have been changed.

Cover photo: Boundary Street, November 12, 1926.
Pittsburgh City Photographer Collection,
1901-2002, AIS.1971.05, Archives Service Center,
University of Pittsburgh.

Frontispiece: Quadri.
Photo courtesy of Raffaele D'Amico.

ISBN 978-0-692-06742-0

Boundary Street Publishing

Kickstarter Publishers

Susan Anderson

Paula Antonelli

Mark & Carolyn Arends

Ron Barry

The Buday Family

Brianne Mitchell

Justine Olawsky

Tricia Walker

Printed in the United States of America.
First Edition 2018.

"The story of any one of us is in some
measure the story of us all."

– Frederick Buechner, *The Sacred Journey*

For Mom and Sara,
and in memory of Ada.

Contents

Foreword

The story of the Italian people is one of tenacity and resilience. Since the seventeenth century, Italians have left their homeland seeking opportunities to establish a new life in the United States. The first Italian diaspora saw more than four million people leave Italy for the United States from the late 1800s through the 1920s. Millions of farmers and tradesmen, many of whom were single, risked everything in search of work, doing anything that would support them and sustain the families they would eventually establish in the new world. Although they all left home for the same reason—to escape the crushing poverty that seemed to have an intractable grip on their homeland—they arrived on our shores with four million different dreams of a promising future.

Once they exited the immigration lines at Ellis Island, they were on their way to make their dreams a reality.

Their stories are strikingly similar. Families typically sent older male children to the United States to work and to find suitable places to eventually start families and begin building a future. These young immigrants toiled in the bleakest of circumstances, laboring for very little pay. What they did earn was mostly sent home in remittances to the loved ones they had left behind.

After years of working and saving, many of these men returned home to marry and to bring their wives back to the United States to establish permanent roots. These women shared the indomitable spirit that had sustained their husbands, and they immediately began the hard work of building homes and families in an unfamiliar language and culture. Those of us who share Italian roots carry this same spirit within us. Just as we are tied to our ancestors, we are equally and sometimes inexplicably connected to others with whom we share this Italian heritage.

Rosemary Capanna and I grew up together in a small town outside Pittsburgh. Although we have known each other for a long time, we seem to have been friends forever. I had never given much thought to that feeling until now. After reading this book, I know exactly what I had never been able to put my finger on.

Set in and around Pittsburgh in the early 1920s, *Beginning on Boundary* is both a historical novel and a love story to the D'Arcangelos of Quadri. Through her meticulous genealogical and historical research, Rosemary introduces us to the story of her grandparents and her mother. The tale was hauntingly familiar because this is the Pittsburgh of my grandparents, too. My own family began life in the United States in the 1920s, when my grandfather, Atilio Natali, left Pistoia in northern Italy with his young wife, Theresa, and their two eldest children. *Beginning on Boundary* is the immigrant story Rosemary and I grew up hearing. As children, we daydreamed about what life must have been like almost a hundred years ago when our grandparents had left behind everything that was familiar to start fresh in the sooty shadows of Pittsburgh's steel mills. We learned the names of the ships upon which they had sailed into New York harbor and imagined the squalid conditions they had endured for weeks at sea. Their stories were imprinted on us at an early age and formed much of the worldview we have today.

If we learned anything from these family stories, it was that no matter how difficult the circumstances, there is always a way. Like millions of other immigrant families, we believed that with tenacity and hard work, most anything was possible. We were humbled by the deep sacrifices that our ancestors had made so that we could access the opportunities afforded in the United States. This shared ancestry, these stories, and this genetic memory explain what has until now been inexplicable.

Jeanne B. Natali, Ph. D.
Director of Intercultural Learning
Tidewater Community College
Norfolk, VA
February 2018

Acknowledgments

My dear friend, James Corrie, agreed to meet me in his spare time and help me retrieve and photocopy my mother's records from Orphan's Court at the Allegheny County Courthouse in Pittsburgh. Circumstances prevented us from doing that for several months, and in the interim, Jim was hired by Allegheny County and began working at the Courthouse. In another of the many strange "coincidences" that occurred during the writing of this book, he was then transferred out of his division to Orphan's Court for several weeks. During their free time (and on their own dime), Jim and his colleague, Frank Morris, researched and photocopied not only the records that I'd requested but Civil Court proceedings, too. Their interest, dedication, and hard work confirmed my mom's recollections and filled in the gaps regarding key players and their motivations over the fight for my grandparents' estate. I owe Jim and Frank a debt of gratitude that is difficult to overstate – without their expertise, I couldn't have told this story nor answered longtime questions about what had happened to my mother.

In 2014, after more than sixty years, Mom was reunited with her paternal first cousin, Ada DeAngelo Pifferetti. Ada delighted in telling me stories about my great uncle (her father, Nicola) and her family, and I delighted in hearing them. Sadly, Ada passed away before the completion of this book. I love her and miss her dearly.

My cousin Raffaele D'Amico researched my mom's paternal and maternal lines in Quadri. He also sent me invaluable photographs and gave me permission to use them. Another cousin, Danilo Coccia, photographed Via di Mezzo. Regular Skype sessions with my cousins Vincenzo D'Aloisio and his wife Letizia Casasanta, as well as the continued email and social media interactions with my Quadresi family, keep me ever-mindful of the importance of our present connection to our past.

My childhood friend and former WPCB colleague, Cindy Chester Moran, was employed by WQED television in Pittsburgh and put me in touch with Tonia Caruso. Tonia produced a wonderful feature on Panther Hollow for their *OnQ* television program, which brought Boundary Street to life for me.

Another WPCB friend, Bill Rhoades, introduced me to Antonella Roione, who graciously and patiently interpreted letters and government forms for me, all the way from her home in Italy. Antonella also provided insight into those translations, as well as the Italian mindset, culture, and lifestyle.

Thanks to Sally Wiggin for the retweet.

Thanks for the helping hand(s): Margaret Becker, Brianne Mitchell, Jeanne Natali, Mary Rutherford-Mihalina, Sharleen Mihalina, Frank Kurtik, Miriam Meislik, Cindy Arnold, and Tony Mariscotti.

Carla Anderton referred me to my easygoing and kind editor, Michael Dell.

Thanks to Pete and Tammy Capanna – my favorite brother and sister-in-law.

My lifelong friend and attorney Lisa J. Buday patiently explained legal terms to me – and never charged a cent.

Ashley Cleveland generously permitted me to use her social media to promote my Kickstarter campaign.

Carolyn and Mark Arends are cherished friends who've seen fit to support and encourage me in ways that defy my understanding. Carolyn personally and wholeheartedly promoted my Kickstarter campaign on her social media, among other things. She also suggested that Mom's story might make a good novel, which caused me to look at the material in a different way and influenced its writing. Thanks so much.

Without Aunt Sara and cousin Patty, this story would've been incomplete. Thank you for letting me include you.

My deepest appreciation to everyone who expressed enthusiasm and interest in this effort, from social media friends to the gentleman who asked why I was filming on Pier Street. Your attentiveness kept me motivated. I noticed, and am indebted to you.

What others are saying about Beginning on Boundary...

"Rosemary Capanna's quest to reconstruct her orphaned mother's history uncovered a riveting family story of immigrant dreams, fierce love, heart-breaking loss, and, eventually, beautiful 'coincidence.' In Beginning on Boundary, Rosemary brings these long-lost relatives and bygone-eras vividly back to life. I could not put this book down, and now Giuseppe, Rosa, Antonio, and Margaret have become a part of my life, too."

- Carolyn Arends, recording artist, author, and Renovaré Director of Education

"Based in Pittsburgh, PA, Beginning on Boundary weaves its way through the streets of Panther Hollow and Oakland and straight into your heart. This incredible account of heartache, loss, and triumph will leave you wanting more – much more. Grab your tissues and get ready for a tale spun so thickly in local history and emotion that it will be hard to put down once you've finished reading."

- Brianne Mitchell, award-winning *Della* and *Lila* book series

"A wonderful journey chronicling an Italian immigrant family through the late 1800s to present day. The early twentieth century brought with it many inequities, and this family seems to have suffered them all. Interesting read."

- Margaret Becker, recording artist/producer

1. The D'Arcangelo Brothers

Quadri is located three hours directly east of Rome. The rugged Gran Sasso d'Italia mountains, part of the Apennines range that runs vertically through Italy, borders Quadri to the west, and the Adriatic Sea lies to its east. The village, or *comune*, is nestled in the heart of the Sangro River valley, which is notable for a 300-foot waterfall and its surrounding craggy, snow-capped mountain peaks. Quadri's main tourist attraction is the annual Truffle Festival, which draws visitors from all over the nation. The festival features a variety of appetizing dishes prepared with truffles, demonstrations of trained dogs that sniff out the delicacy, and tours of historical ruins. There are traditional folk concerts and a vintage photographic display at the town's historical center. People also come to shop, perusing the wares of many craftsmen and vendors.

In the late 1800s, prospects were much dimmer. Most Quadresi subsisted as peasant farmers, *contadini*, eking out meager existences. They'd grow just enough food to feed their families. If the harvest was good, the bounty was sold at market, generating a small income.

America was a distant dream, a faraway land bordering on mythical proportions. There, a hardworking man could find a decent job and make enough money to support his family, perhaps buy a house and offer a better life to his descendants. *The land of opportunity*, it was proclaimed. Families scrimped and saved enough to purchase a train ticket to the nearest port and then steerage on a ship bound for the *New Country*. The eldest son went first. Usually a cousin, another relative, or a close friend was already established and provided room and board and helped with the job search. Once the oldest son was employed, he'd send his family a small amount of money from each paycheck. The next son would save it and then make the same journey – and so on and so on, right down the line. Perhaps the parents would eventually emigrate too, although most did not. Men arrived in America and never saw their parents or extended families – or the *Old Country* – again.

During the Age of Mass Migration (1850-1913), a period of open borders, thirty million immigrants entered the United States; from 1880 to 1915, an estimated thirteen million Italians migrated out of Italy, making it the scene of the largest voluntary emigration in recorded world history.[1] Four million of those immigrants arrived in the United States, the majority from 1900 to 1914.[2] Among them were four of the six sons of Quadri's Sebastiano D'Arcangelo and Fedele Di Pilato: Nicola, Sebastiano, Giuseppe, and Gennaro.

Nicola, who was born in 1884, arrived in 1900 when he was barely sixteen years old. He joined some cousins in Canonsburg, PA, and was soon working in the town's large tin mill. His name was Anglicized, and he became known as "Nick DeAngelo." Nick worked for four years, faithfully sending money to his family in Quadri. Then, Sebastiano (born in 1887) came next in 1904. His name was Anglicized to "Mike DeAngelo." Mike made the trip to Canonsburg but eventually moved south to Fayette County, PA, where he became a railroader. Although slightly out of chronological order, Gennaro (born in 1891), who was younger than Giuseppe, made the journey at the age of eighteen in 1910. He, too, went to Nicola's house in

Canonsburg, but he quickly made his way to cousins in eastern Washington County, who resided in the small town of East Pike Run Township (California), PA. There, he became a coal miner, and was known as "Charlie Angelo."

Giuseppe's growing romance with Rosa D'Aloisio may have made him reluctant to leave Quadri, surrendering his turn to Charlie. Giuseppe and Rosa were married in 1909, when he was twenty and she was twenty-one.

"Rosa, please don't cry. It'll be OK. Nicola and Sebastiano say that in a few years, I'll make more than enough money to buy you a ticket to America, too. It's not much time at all. Things are getting worse, and I can't scrape enough money together for us. I want a better life, don't you?"

Giuseppe D'Arcangelo's words were heartfelt, but they were of little consolation to his wife. After only four years of marriage – and a lifetime of friendship – Giuseppe had decided to make his way to America in 1913. At barely twenty-four years old, he couldn't bear the thought of scratching out an existence in the mountainous terrain of Quadri. His family was comprised of peasants and farmers. That's the way it had been for generations, but now there was an opportunity to do better. Why should his children and grandchildren be expected to toil so hard to just survive? He wanted them to *live*. To make matters worse, there was political upheaval, and Italy's economy was collapsing. Three of his brothers had already made the crossing and were doing well. They wrote him lengthy letters about their new lives and jobs. Yes, the hours were long, and the work was exhausting, but the pay was good. People were friendly, all striving to carve out a better future for themselves and their descendants. His brothers implored him to join them.

Domenico D'Arcangelo and Fedele Di Pilato (pictured) raised six sons in their home in Quadri: Nicola, Sebastiano, Giuseppe, Gennaro, Ermete, and Aquilino. Ermete and Aquilino remained in Quadri. Photo of Fedele's house courtesy of Raffaele D'Amico.

"I'll never see you again," Rosa said.

"That's silly. You'll see me again – sooner than you can imagine. If I get there and it isn't everything I've been told, I'll work for a while and move back home. I'll make enough money for us to live better here, like some of our cousins have done."

Rosa knew Giuseppe's mind was set. Despite her apprehension, she supported his decision, and her excitement slowly grew. She realized that he was smart, one of the smartest young men in the comune. He carefully weighed his options and was never rash. Even though his brothers sent money for his passage and would have sent more for pocket money, Giuseppe conscientiously farmed additional land and marketed the extra harvest, and he bred goats and sold them. He was able to save $26 to take with him to America. Rosa understood that he was determined, and his enthusiasm was contagious.

Giuseppe was excited and a little nervous about the trip. He grasped that it would take a great deal of hard work and sacrifice to be successful wherever they made their life. America was an entire ocean away. He had never traveled before, certainly had never gone much farther than fifteen or twenty miles from Quadri. He thought about the small comune and how everyone was connected. Families lived in the town for generations; his own line was established in the village in 1660, when his great-great grandfather, also named Giuseppe D'Arcangelo, moved from Borrello to Quadri with his wife, Angela Di Nardo. Everyone pulled together, especially when times were hard. He knew that Rosa would be cared for in his absence.

"It'll be wonderful," he said. "Eventually we'll have our own house. We have a lot of family and friends there already…it'll seem like home."

"We'll see. I'm going to miss you so much."

"Me too, Rosa."

Top photo: The back of Rosa's house (circled) at 40 Via di Mezzo from a 1934 picture postcard.
Bottom photo: The front of Rosa's house (left) in 2018.
Postcard and photo courtesy of Raffaele D'Amico.

Rosa was worried about the voyage, but she was comforted that her uncle, Sebastiano D'Aloisio, was traveling with Giuseppe. Sebastiano was forty-eight and had lived in America for ten years (1896-1906), so he understood the complexities of international travel. They would take the train from Napoli to the Port of Le Havre, France, then set sail on April 9. They'd reach Halifax, Nova Scotia, in about a week. Once there, they'd work for a while on the railroad and visit with family in Centerville, Ontario. After a three-month stay, they planned to cross the border into the United States and travel to Buffalo, NY. Sebastiano would stay in Buffalo and visit with family for several more months before returning to Italy. Giuseppe would finish the last leg of his journey to Canonsburg, PA, to join his brother, Nick.

The ocean voyage was rough, as they sailed across the North Atlantic on the *Niagara* in early spring. Hundreds were jammed into steerage, and the smell was overwhelming. However, Giuseppe rarely ventured on deck for fresh air; he was too ill. Sebastiano kept a close eye on him. Almost a year earlier, to the day, the Titanic had sunk in these very waters, and the passengers knew it. At first, each roll and tilt of the ship sent a collective gasp through the group, but after a week, most were oblivious to it.

They arrived in Halifax on April 17. Giuseppe and Sebastiano traveled by train and entered Ontario through the Port of Montreal. They were greeted by family, and they got to work almost immediately. Giuseppe endured the backbreaking work on the railroad, but decided it wasn't for him. To his credit, he'd saved even more money – now he had $50 to take with him to America. Although he enjoyed visiting with cousins he hadn't seen in several years, he was anxious to get to Nick's place and begin the new life he envisioned for himself, Rosa, and, hopefully, their large family. He caught a train to Canonsburg as soon as he could.

Nick was now twenty-nine and married to Carmela D'Amico, also of Quadri. He worked almost non-stop and was able to purchase a large house on Giffin Avenue. There was an apartment upstairs that included a kitchen. Giuseppe lived there until he found work, happily preparing himself spaghetti or other simple dishes, but mostly dining with Nick and Carmela and enjoying their company. Before long, and due to their connections in the Italian community, he was hired by Jones and Laughlin (J&L) Steel as a laborer in the pipe mill in Hazelwood, PA. He settled in Panther Hollow in the Oakland section of Pittsburgh, where many of his cousins and friends lived. Giuseppe first boarded with a distant cousin, Giovanni Sciulli, at 389 Boundary Street. Giovanni, or John, also worked at J&L. Most of the men on Boundary Street did. They would take the long walk down Boundary to the mill that sat in the flats along the Monongahela River on Second Avenue. The steel mill was hot, dirty, and physically demanding work, but the good wages made it bearable. Giuseppe's English improved so much that his accent was almost unnoticeable, and soon the foremen and managers took note.

When Rosa's first cousin, Albericio "Albert" Pacella, proposed that they board together at 15 Boundary, Giuseppe accepted. Albert had arrived in America a year before Giuseppe and was working as a pipe liner with a company out of Fairmont, West Virginia. Giuseppe briefly considered a career change, but he decided the steel industry afforded him more opportunities for advancement.

As Giuseppe labored in the dangerous mill, picking up extra shifts whenever he could, Rosa scrimped and saved what he sent home to her. She dreamed of her journey to America, longing to join her husband and begin their family.

Unfortunately, as with many men who fled Italy to avoid conscription, Giuseppe and his brother Charlie found themselves caught up in the horror of World War One. In 1918, Charlie was drafted and sent to Camp Sherman in Ohio, and then he was quickly shipped off to Europe. He notably fought in the Battle of the Argonne Forest in France, attaining the rank of corporal. He returned home with tattooed forearms, tangible evidence of his sacrifice and service to his beloved adopted homeland. One arm featured Lady Columbia and the other Lady Liberty. He was a proud charter member of the California, PA, American Legion.

Giuseppe, who was two years older than Charlie, was drafted later and avoided another transatlantic crossing. He spent eight months in Camp Lee, VA. When influenza swept through the troops in late 1918, he miraculously avoided illness. His time at boot camp was uneventful, except for one very important thing: To acknowledge the participation of immigrants, the US government briefly allowed military personnel to become naturalized citizens during their enlistment, foregoing the traditional waiting period. Giuseppe filled out the form, took the oath, and the Circuit Court of the Eastern District of Virginia (Richmond) declared him a US citizen on the spot. During this short window, these declarations were also derivative, which meant that Rosa became a US citizen, too, simply through her marriage to Giuseppe. She had yet to set foot in America but was immediately afforded all the rights of an American citizen.

The War to End All Wars interrupted Giuseppe's life in Pittsburgh, but he was honored to have served. When he returned, he bore down even harder at J&L and began working two or three shifts at a time. He was popular among his friends and co-workers, so much so that when a foreman position opened at the mill, they encouraged him to apply. He did, and soon "Joseph Angelo" was guiding a crew of men through the steel-making process. Through it all, he and Rosa wrote each other faithfully. He sent money home and told her to save just a little for her passage and to use the rest to help both their families. She heeded her caring husband's message (the extra money that came from all the D'Arcangelo brothers in America made life a bit easier for those who remained in Quadri). Of course, this generosity, coupled with the interruption of WWI, meant that it took Rosa longer to save what was needed, so it wasn't until 1923 that she'd finally put aside enough money to pay for her ticket to America – a full ten years after Giuseppe departed for the United States.

Giuseppe D'Arcangelo and Albericio Pacella (Albert Pascell)
boarded together at 15 Boundary Street.

2. Giuseppe and Rosa

Rosa had been preparing for her move to America for ten years, but it was still a bit of a shock when the time finally came to say goodbye to her family and friends. It all seemed so final, and Rosa felt the enormity of leaving Quadri, perhaps forever. She tucked away a few family photos, some pieces of clothing, and a delicate handkerchief that her mother, Domenica, had crocheted for her into her bag. Giuseppe told her not to bring much, that she could shop in America for new clothes that would help her fit in with the other women. She enjoyed being as fashionable as possible, even though they had little, so the chance to shop in a big city was appealing. He wrote about how Pittsburgh teemed with life, even at night. The air was filled with smoke from the non-stop churning of the steel mills, and the skies glowed red. People filled the streets, and there were cars and trolleys…the stories made her head spin with wonderment and joy.

While Giuseppe's descriptions of American life thrilled Rosa and she was more than ready to be with him, an unexplainable fear had been bothering her for months. She didn't understand why, and that troubled her even more. She had long, quiet talks with her mother, who tried to calm her doubts. Domenica wanted a better life for her daughter and grandchildren than Italy offered, and although she knew she would miss Rosa, she believed she would see her again.

"Mama, what if I don't come back? What if I never see you and Papa again?"

"You'll visit. You'll bring your children to meet us. Giuseppe told me this, and I believe him."

"I'm not as sure as you, Mama."

"You always were the one to worry." Domenica laughed softly. "So many serious thoughts in such a young mind."

"I'm not so young anymore, Mama. Giuseppe and I have been married for fourteen years. I haven't seen him in ten."

Domenica gently nodded, leaned in, and took Rosa's hand. "Life is like a river. It flows where it wants and makes its way however it likes. We can't control it, so we must learn to live with it. Perhaps God will bring you back. If he doesn't, we must accept it."

Rosa knew her mother was right. She and Giuseppe loved each other, and their commitment to one another had withstood the time and distance between them.

That evening, she took a final stroll through the comune, promising herself that she would remember everything about Quadri so that she could one day tell her children about it, in case they never returned to visit.

Early the next morning, her brother, Vincenzo, accompanied her on the three-hour train ride to Napoli, where she would board the ship that would carry her to the United States. When they finally reached the city, they were surprised to see markers directing emigrants to the port. So many people were leaving Italy that the authorities decided to help facilitate the process; it was better than finding stranded people who had missed their ship and lost the ticket fee they'd scrimped and saved to pay.

Vincenzo found the correct ship, the *Giulio Cesare*. The pier buzzed with people and cartage.

"Well, here we are. Let me see your ticket again. Yes, August first, 1923. Do you have the instructions Giuseppe wrote in English about which train to take to Pittsburgh? He said that if you have any problems just show the paper to a policeman. He sent you the ticket too, right?"

"Yes, the instructions and ticket are in my purse."

"Don't forget to write, Rosa. Mama will be upset if she doesn't hear from you often."

"Oh no, I won't forget. How could I?"

Rosa hesitated, reluctant to leave. She'd never been to Napoli, let alone on a ship. She was about to spend ten days sailing to New York. Rosa suddenly felt like a tiny speck on a very large world.

Vincenzo sensed her indecision. "Do you want to give me your ticket?" he joked. "Giuseppe will be happy to see me, but not as happy as he'll be when he sees you."

That was all Rosa needed to hear. She threw her arms around Vincenzo, hugging him as tightly as she could.

"Goodbye, Vincenzo. I'll write as soon as I can. Write back to me and tell me all about what's happening in Quadri. I love you."

"I will. I love you, too, Rosa."

Vincenzo watched as she hiked up the steep gangplank, her small suitcase in one hand, the other holding the rail. He wiped tears from his eyes and turned to begin his long, lonely journey home.

While Rosa didn't know anyone on the ship, she was the quiet type, unassuming and not given to gossip or any sort of idle chatter. She had a small, private room, but she tolerated it by remembering she would only be using it for ten days. Rosa had a crochet hook and some yarn, and she busied herself making small projects, such as gloves or hats, and then unravelling them and starting over. When she was bored with that, she walked the deck, breathing in the fresh salt air and marveling at the ocean's enormity. Surprisingly, she didn't get seasick. She enjoyed walking, although she missed the scenery the countryside afforded. The nights were harder. She barely slept due to the anticipation of finally being reunited with Giuseppe. All sorts of thoughts raced through her mind. She worried they might not recognize each other after so many years, or perhaps he had become too "Americanized" to appreciate her simple ways. After all, he was a foreman now, an important man. What if she couldn't adapt? He told her he was fluent in English; she only knew a few words. It seemed they were so different. How would they overcome this?

"It's too late to turn back now," she told herself repeatedly.

One day, word went out that they were close to New York, so Rosa went on deck. She walked the perimeter of the ship as it steamed into New York Harbor, and she heard excited cheers.

"*La Signora! La Statua della Libertà!*"

Rosa hurried toward the bow and stared in amazement at the Statue of Liberty.

She thought to herself, *The Lady welcomes us to our new home, while she looks to the old.* As she stood and gazed at the monument, she was surprised to find herself weeping. Rosa was tired from the long journey. She had left the only home she'd ever known to join her husband, whom she hadn't seen in ten years. The Lady's nobility and grace touched something deep inside her, and she had a renewed sense that everything would be all right.

The *Giulio Cesare* docked, and health officers boarded the ship to inspect the fitness of the first- and second-class passengers. Since she was a US citizen who held a second-class ticket, the health inspector released her quickly, and she was on her way.

Rosa showed Giuseppe's instructions to translators who were stationed throughout the port, and they guided her to the correct train. She was wary and afraid; she'd never seen so many people before, and all of them were in a hurry. She had to wait a few hours for the train, but it soon arrived, and Rosa began the final leg of her journey to

Pittsburgh. She relaxed, and the rhythm of the train lulled her into a sound sleep.

The train jolting to a stop woke Rosa up. The conductor shouted, "Pittsburgh!" She sleepily tried to collect her thoughts and remembered that she was in America. Giuseppe told her the train fare included lunch, but she had slept through it.

Now, all she had to do was collect her bag and wait for Giuseppe to find her.

As she left the train, Rosa scanned the terminal for a bench to await his arrival. It was Saturday, so the station wasn't too busy. She noticed a tall man to her right, staring at her and smiling. She realized it was Giuseppe, and she ran to him. They embraced and shared a passionate kiss.

"You made it! I know you're tired. Don't worry. I've got a nice place set up for us. You can bathe and then sleep for days, if you like."

"Beppe...I can't believe I'm here. You look so healthy!" Rosa noticed that Giuseppe had put on some weight and was no longer the skinny, almost boyish young man she last saw ten years ago; he had grown up.

Giuseppe laughed. "Oh yeah, I'm healthy. The entire neighborhood makes sure I'm well-fed. It's a good thing, too. I work so much that I can barely fix myself a plate of spaghetti *aglio e olio*! Come on, let's go. We'll talk all about it after you've rested."

3. Boundary Street

Giuseppe and Rosa rode the trolley as far as they could to South Oakland. Rosa noticed the homes were larger and newer than any she'd ever seen. They walked a few blocks down Bouquet, then came to the steeply declining Joncaire, which was paved with brick. Down they went, straight into Panther Hollow, where finally they reached Boundary Street. Rosa saw the street sign and recognized the name; it was the address she had written countless times when corresponding with Giuseppe. Unlike Joncaire, Boundary wasn't paved and there weren't any sidewalks. Mud was everywhere. Some boards were strategically placed over the worst spots, but they were slick and wet. It was a careful balancing act, but Giuseppe held her hand and guided her.

At last, they stopped in front of a blue, three-story house.

"Here we are," Giuseppe said proudly.

Rosa was impressed. The house was tall, long, and new.

"We're renting the back – 40 Rear. We have all three floors. This is the best place for us. Walk up Joncaire and it's a different world – suddenly, you're in the city, and it's all noise and traffic. You'll see. But this little hollow is quiet and isolated. I can walk to the mill in about fifteen minutes, so it's close to work. Best of all, everyone who lives here is from Quadri, Pizzoferrato, or Gamberale, so we're related to most of them. I have a garden in Giovanni Sciulli's empty lot just down the street. Everybody shares and watches out for one another, just like back home. In some ways, it's like I've never left Quadri. I know I wrote you about all this, but I want to reassure you. You're going to love Pittsburgh, Rosa. It's a great place to make our home and raise our family."

40 Boundary Street. Antonio and Rose D'Amico lived in the front (top photo). Giuseppe and Rosa D'Arcangelo lived in the rear apartment, closest to the steps (bottom photo).

Rosa smiled. Giuseppe's attention to detail had never wavered, and he was still the thoughtful and kind person she had fallen in love with when they were children. His excitement was endearing; he wanted her to appreciate the New World as much as he did.

"I'm sure you're right, Beppe."

"Come on, I'll show you the place. I know you want to sleep. It's been a long trip."

Giuseppe opened the door to a small kitchen. A little further in was a living room. The bathroom was off to one side. There were two large bedrooms upstairs. The duplex was new and clean and perfectly sized for them.

Rosa bathed and crawled into bed, exhausted but relieved to be with Giuseppe. She felt better about being in America when she saw how healthy and happy he was and the wonderful home he'd prepared for her. She'd spent a lot of time in Quadri worrying about him. He was a hard worker, the type who would neglect himself to earn income. Although he had been drafted five years ago, he didn't seem any worse for it. She was aware of the worldwide influenza epidemic in 1918 – some of their family in Quadri died from complications, and Giuseppe had written her about the infections at Camp Lee. He didn't get sick, but some of his friends had. Several of them died.

She wondered why her mind wandered like this. *I'm too serious-minded, like Mama says*, she thought. She turned over in bed and noticed Giuseppe sitting in the corner.

"Beppe?" she said softly.

"Sleep, Rosa. I'm so glad you're here. I love you."

"I love you, too."

Rosa awoke Sunday morning around ten. Giuseppe brought her a cup of coffee and some biscotti.

"Breakfast in bed, just like a real American," he said. "When you're finished, get dressed, and I'll show you around the neighborhood."

"Oh, Beppe. There's so much mud!"

"Don't worry, it dried out quite a bit overnight. I cleaned your shoes for you, so you won't be embarrassed because they're dirty."

Giuseppe grinned. He knew his wife was fastidious and took pride in her appearance. He took pride in his, too. As a foreman at Jones and Laughlin Steel, he desired to set an example for the young men who were ambitious and wanted to make their way in America. If he could do it, so could they.

Rosa finished her breakfast, dressed, and met Giuseppe in the kitchen.

"It's hot," Rosa said.

"Not as bad as Quadri in the summer."

"Yes, but at least there's a breeze in Quadri!"

He grabbed her hand and escorted her out the door. Even though the August humidity was almost unbearable, the streets had dried and were passable. They walked around the Hollow, and Rosa was encouraged to see many familiar faces. Giuseppe was right; it was almost as though they'd never left Quadri. She found cousins and distant cousins and many friends who'd established themselves and were now raising children. Some, to her amazement, had encouraged their parents to emigrate. Extended families were happily crammed into little houses. Children played in the streets, and it seemed that everyone was making sauce for Sunday dinner.

Giuseppe walked Rosa down Boundary and showed her Panther Hollow Lake. They continued walking, all the way down to the mill, the sheer size of which astounded Rosa.

"You ought to see it when we're working. It's all smoke and fire."

"How safe is this?"

"It's safer now that I'm a foreman. I'm responsible for my crew, so I make sure they're safe, too."

"I would get lost inside there."

"I used to feel the same way, but I had friends who showed me. I learned. Speaking of which, we'll make sure you learn some English. I don't want you to be stuck at home all the time when I'm working. It's not hard to get around. You can walk, or take the trolley."

Rosa was always adventurous, hiking into the mountains back home and walking as far as she could to explore her surroundings. She hoped to do the same in Pittsburgh, and now Giuseppe was encouraging her to do just that.

"There are plenty of stores downtown, so you'll be able to pick up a few things. You don't have to worry about grocery shopping too much – you won't have to go far. There are two stores in the Hollow, and a lot more in Oakland. One's right above us on Bouquet. Plus, we'll can whatever I grow in my garden."

"But where will we store those jars, Beppe?"

"We have a cellar! Well, half a cellar. I can put up shelves. I asked the landlord, and he told me it was fine. His son is on my mill crew."

Giuseppe and Rosa visited with family and friends and had dinner with their cousins, the D'Amicos. Rosa felt a tinge of homesickness but was having fun.

The next week, she and her distant cousin, Giulia, walked downtown. Giulia knew all the shops and helped Rosa purchase two nice dresses and a hat that matched both. She also bought a pair of dress shoes. Her everyday clothes would suffice for now, but she wanted to dress appropriately for mass and other formal occasions.

Rosa felt extravagant, but she and Giuseppe were careful with their finances. He was working double shifts and overtime and making good money, but they had plans that required them to save. They had long discussions about buying a home, having children, and sending them to college. Their children would have better lives and not work long, hard, dangerous hours in a steel mill or coal mine. They talked about how their children might become teachers or bankers. They dreamed, Giuseppe worked, and Rosa cared for and supported him.

They settled into a contented life. Despite all the hours Giuseppe worked, they made time for mass at least once a week, traveling to the Immaculate Conception parish in Bloomfield, where more of their extended family lived. Giuseppe and his steel mill friends played cards once a week. Rosa and her neighbors learned how to bake bread in their modern gas ovens and spoke "American" to each other. She liked to explore Oakland, taking in the skyscrapers and dodging traffic. Rosa was adapting and feeling more confident about her new life.

One Saturday in the spring, there was a knock on the door. Giuseppe opened it to find his brother, Charlie, grinning at him. It wasn't unusual for Charlie to catch the train from California, PA, to Hazelwood. He'd stay the weekend and take in a Pirates baseball game or two at Forbes Field, which was perched just above them on South Bouquet.

"Well, if it isn't my handsome brother-in-law," Rosa said. "Let me fix you something to eat. Mortadella and fresh bread. That sounds good, right?"

"It does, Rosa. Thank you. Beppe, come to the game with me today. It'll be fun."

"Thanks, but I have to work in the garden."

"I've already started mine."

"I haven't had time until today. We want to do some canning, so I must get to it. Maybe next time. Are you staying the weekend? You should've brought Lena."

"You know her, she doesn't like to go anywhere. I can't stay. I have a fundraiser at the American Legion tomorrow – spaghetti dinner."

"You made Mama's sauce again?"

"They like spaghetti! I don't mind doing it. We almost have the Legion's mortgage paid off."

"That's great. Do you see Mike? He's only ten minutes or so away from you."

"I see him sometimes. The two of you, all you do is work. What about Nick?"

"Yes, we've been to Canonsburg. We usually go on Sundays. We love to see our nieces. They're growing up fast. I took my mandolin once, and Louise played it. She broke a string. The poor girl thought I would be angry. I wasn't. I think she's musical, like us."

Charlie laughed. "I play the cornet in the Legion band. Nick should get her a horn."

He and Giuseppe roared, and Rosa brought them sandwiches.

"Stay for supper, Charlie," she said. "We're having frittata and insalata. There's plenty. We'll have more time to visit. You can take some home to Lena, too."

"OK, I will. The game starts at one and should be over by four, if there aren't extra innings. Last train home leaves at six."

Charlie and Giuseppe dug into their sandwiches and talked about work and family. Rosa listened intently and mused about how some things never seemed to change.

Giuseppe and Rosa itched to start their own family. In 1924, Rosa discovered she was pregnant and that the baby was due in December. Giuseppe could barely contain himself, and Rosa was relieved to know he decided she would deliver the baby at Magee Women's Hospital rather than at home with a midwife, like some of the other women had done. The infant mortality rates in Pittsburgh and Quadri were high; Rosa had lost two sisters and two brothers during infancy. They understood the risks and were going to do everything they could to ensure they brought a healthy firstborn baby into the world.

The happy couple prepared the second bedroom in their home. They were given a crib, and Rosa crocheted baby blankets and clothes. Giuseppe, already the doting husband, was beside himself. He did everything he could to keep Rosa comfortable. They were apart for fourteen years and had only been reunited for two, and now it seemed their dreams and plans were falling into place. They wanted a big family. He was thirty-five and she was thirty-six, not exactly a young age to begin one. Yet, here they were.

December came and went, and Rosa still hadn't delivered the baby. She grew very ill and told Giuseppe that the baby wasn't kicking anymore. Giuseppe called her doctor, and they went to see him at Magee. He examined Rosa, and the concerned expression on his face scared them.

"I'm sorry…I have some terrible news," the doctor said. "The baby is dead but hasn't stopped growing. I don't know what happened, but the child is oversized. We'll have to induce labor immediately. This is a very dangerous situation. We may have to operate."

After the loss of their baby, in her grief, Rosa wrote to her sister-in-law, Lena.

Pittsburgh, February 11th, 1925

Dear sister-in-law,

I am writing this letter to let you know that my husband and I are well, and I will love to hear about my brother-in-law and yourself.

I want you to know that in January I delivered a baby, but because we have bad luck, the baby died, and I was in the hospital three weeks. They weighed him, and he was sixteen pounds. I never thought I would have to experience this, that my baby would die, and we are so sorry about this fact. Now, I must stop writing, please say hello to my brother-in-law Gennaro and to your brothers and your sisters-in-law; for you all, my and my husband's greetings.

Your sister-in-law

Rosa D'Arcangelo

Please answer my few lines. Goodbye and ciao.

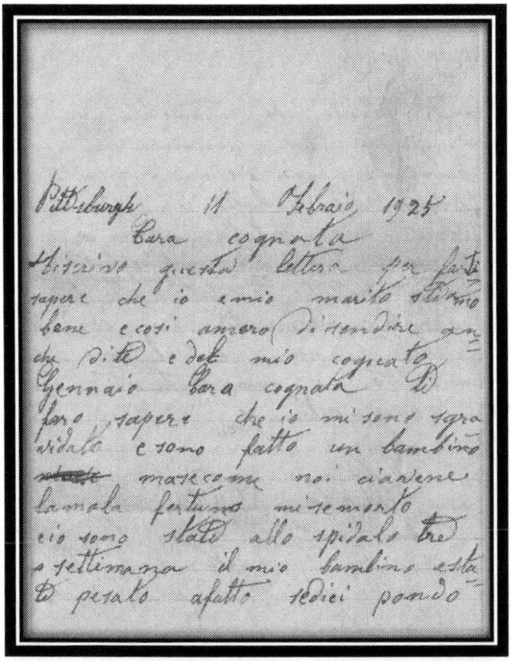

Pittsburgh 11 Febraio 1925
Cara cognata
Ti scrivo questa lettera per farti
sapere che io e mio marito stiamo
bene e così amoro di sendire an
che di te e del mio cognato
Gennaio Cara cognata Di
faro sapere che io mi sono sgra
vidato e sono fatto un bambino
[illegible] masecome noi ciavene
lamala fortuna mi sementato
e io sono stato allo spidale tre
settimana il mio bambino esta
to pesato afatto sedici pondo

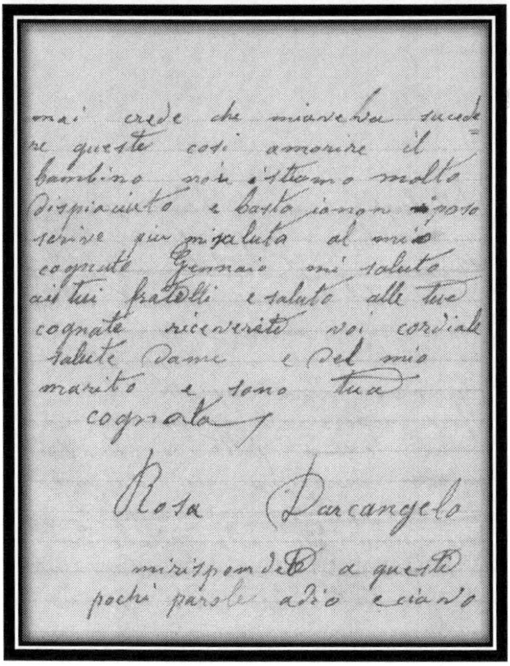

mai crede che mi avevo succede
re questo così amorire il
bambino noi istiamo molto
dispiaciuto e basta ianon miposo
scrivo più mi saluta al mio
cognato Gennaio mi saluto
ai tui fratelli e saluto alle tue
cognate riceverete voi cordiale
salute da me e del mio
marito e sono tua
cognata
Rosa Darcangelo
mirispondete a queste
pochi parole adio e ciao

Rosa's letter describing the birth of her stillborn son.

Rosa, who used a blend of Italian and English when writing her letters, didn't have the words to describe how horrible she felt about the loss of her child. The doctor determined that the umbilical cord was prolapsed, depriving the baby of oxygen and nutrients. He had died of intrauterine asphyxia but continued to grow in Rosa's womb until he reached sixteen pounds. The child, an unnamed boy, was buried in an unmarked grave at St. Peter's Cemetery in the Larimer section of Pittsburgh, while Rosa was still recuperating in the hospital.

Rosa and Giuseppe had wonderful neighbors, who brought them meals and sat with Rosa while Giuseppe continued to work in the mill. The days felt longer, and the last throes of winter seemed harsher than any Rosa had ever experienced. Giuseppe promised that things would get better; the doctor told them to wait a while and then try again. What happened was a rare occurrence; the child was otherwise healthy. It was little consolation to Rosa, but she trusted her husband. She lit candles at church and prayed for their son.

Giuseppe's garden overflowed that year, and they busied themselves with canning. They also had new neighbors. In the late summer of 1925, the front of the duplex was rented to one of Giuseppe's distant cousins from Quadri, Antonio D'Amico. Giuseppe, Rosa, and Antonio were lifelong friends. Antonio's wife, Rose Fagnilli, was born in Pittsburgh, but her parents hailed from Pizzoferrato, just a few short miles from Quadri. They were expecting their first child the coming February.

Antonio also worked in the pipe mill, but not in the same section as Giuseppe. Their proximity would give them opportunities to catch up on family, and they could walk to the mill together when their shifts coincided. Things were beginning to feel normal again on Boundary Street, and Rosa consoled herself with the notion that life did go on. She wasn't the first woman to lose a child, and she could endure this grief if others could.

Sadly, Antonio's wife Rose died during childbirth in February 1926. The baby, a girl, was healthy, but Rose's placenta dropped, and she bled to death in her bedroom in the front duplex apartment. She was twenty-years-old. Antonio was shocked and devastated. After the glorious emotional high over the birth of his daughter, he watched in despair as his wife died. How would he go on without her? How would he care for a child while working in the mill? It felt like too much to bear. Rose's family stepped in and insisted the child be adopted by a cousin and her family. Antonio, in his sorrow, couldn't see a way through the situation. His brothers were in Italy, and he didn't have any close family here to help him. He relented, went to court, and signed the papers. The baby was formally adopted by her cousin. Antonio named her Rose, after her mother.

Giuseppe and Rosa did their best to comfort him, but he was a broken man. He relinquished the apartment he shared with Rose and became a boarder again, this time with yet another distant cousin. Giuseppe routinely sought out Antonio and made sure he wasn't alone too often; they both had lost children and shared a common grief.

The next year, Rosa continued to heal until the doctor declared her physically able to have children. In 1927, Rosa was pregnant again, with the baby due in October. She and Giuseppe were happy, but wary. They didn't want to lose another child. Giuseppe made sure that Rosa received regular checkups, ate well, and got plenty of rest. He wasn't taking any chances.

On November 1, 1927, their daughter, Margherita Rosa, was born in Magee Women's Hospital. The birth went smoothly, and the baby was healthy. She was the answer to their hopes and prayers. They were a small family, but a family nonetheless. Rosa was almost forty, and they probably wouldn't have any more children because of the health risks involved. They decided to pour everything they had into Margherita.

Giuseppe was a loving, involved father. He was working more than ever, excited by the prospect of having to provide for a newborn. One day in the summer of 1928, he quietly told Rosa he had managed to save $5000, a small fortune equal to roughly $70,000 in today's dollars. Soon, they would buy a house where they could raise their daughter, perhaps out in the suburbs. Panther Hollow was a good place to live, but the duplex would start to feel cramped with a toddler. Rosa understood. She was proud of his thriftiness and excited at the thought of having her own home.

In October 1928, for Margherita's first birthday that was coming up in November, Giuseppe and Rosa decided to have a portrait made. They corresponded regularly with their family in Quadri, but this year Giuseppe had a baby to show off, and he wanted to send photos to them. Rosa eagerly agreed, and the family sat for its singular portrait.

Rosa continued to try to talk Giuseppe into slowing down. With their savings and his position at the mill, he didn't have to work so much. But Giuseppe cared about his crew and didn't feel right about expecting them to work long hours if he didn't.

"You're older than they are," Rosa said. "You've saved so much money. You don't have to do this."

"Rosa, you don't understand. I must work hard to set an example for my men and to keep providing for us. Besides, I'm not the only foreman. Someone else could take my place. I don't want to work in the mines or on the railroad. I'm too old for that. This job suits me. I'll be able to slow down in a few more years. You'll see."

Rosa knew she wouldn't be able to talk him into slowing down now. That winter, she noticed him coughing.

"Beppe, maybe you should see the doctor. Your cough is getting worse."

Giuseppe, Margherita, and Rosa. It's believed this photo was taken around the time of Margherita's first birthday in November 1928. Giuseppe died a few months later.

"I'll have a little more wine later, and I'll be OK. It's just a cold. I have to leave now, or I'll be late for work."

"Please see the doctor."

"OK. If I have time, I will. Bye, Rosa. I'll see you a little later."

Giuseppe's cough developed into chest congestion. He continued to work, believing he would get through it. But his immune system was weakened, and on January 25, 1929, he was diagnosed with the flu. It was a time before antibiotics, when aspirin was prescribed for everything, although it only reduced fever and held aches and pains at bay. The doctor who attended him told him to stay in bed, but Giuseppe refused to believe that it was serious. Rosa was dismayed that he wouldn't stop working. Finally, his body gave out. He couldn't get out of bed, and he was diagnosed with bilateral pneumonia.

Rosa sent a telegram to Charlie, imploring him to come quickly to the house on Boundary. Charlie arrived and was able to talk with his brother for a few days, until he lapsed into unconsciousness.

On Sunday, February 3, 1929, at 6:00 a.m., just nine days after his initial diagnosis and with Rosa, Margherita, and Charlie by his side, Giuseppe died. He was thirty-nine-years-old.

4. Antonio and Rosa

Rosa felt as though she couldn't breathe. She and Giuseppe had been reunited briefly, just six years, but the future had looked promising. They had a child and plans. She thought the heartache might be too much to bear and wept inconsolably. Rosa was now alone in America with an infant. Although Giuseppe had left a nest egg, she worried about what she would do once it was gone. Certainly, it wasn't enough to last a lifetime in America. What would become of her and Margherita? Should she return to Italy?

Family and friends did all they could to help. Charlie sent telegrams, not only to his brothers in Brownsville and Canonsburg, but to his parents in Quadri, too. A cousin from Quadri who was living in Pittsburgh's Hill District, Joseph D'Amico, suggested Giuseppe be buried in his family plot at Calvary Catholic Cemetery in Hazelwood, where his daughter, Mary Louise, had been laid to rest. She'd contracted measles when she was just one-and-a-half years old and passed away in 1927.

Rosa was too distraught to make decisions, so family made them for her. Thankfully, she didn't have to endure the agony of selecting a plot for her young husband. After a wake at the house on Boundary Street, Giuseppe was buried next to Mary Louise on February 5. Many of his co-workers were in attendance, along with most of the neighborhood. Antonio D'Amico, who continued to live in the Hollow after his young wife had died a few years earlier, took the day off to say goodbye to his cousin and close friend. He comforted Rosa and assured her that he would help however he could.

The house at 40 Boundary, which had held so much hope, began to feel as though it was cursed. In the span of Rosa's short six years there, Giuseppe and Rosa's firstborn died, Antonio's wife died, and now Giuseppe was lost. The house held painful memories, but there were good ones, too. Giuseppe, ever true to his word, had built the shelves in the basement, which were filled with jars of vegetables from his garden. His coat hung neatly on the peg in the kitchen, and his lunch bucket was tucked under the sink. The house felt horribly empty, yet strangely full. Rosa wondered if she would ever be happy again.

The women in the neighborhood took turns watching Margherita, giving Rosa time to grieve. Antonio dropped in occasionally. They chatted about Giuseppe and Quadri. So much had changed in such a short time, and the similarities of their experiences and situations weren't lost on them. Each had lost a spouse and a child. And Antonio was still grieving, too. As if the pain of losing his wife wasn't enough, he had to endure the ache of not being permitted to have any contact with his daughter. Sometimes he caught a distant glimpse of her if the cousins came to the Hollow to visit family. Rose's family blamed him for her death; if he hadn't gotten her pregnant, she wouldn't have died. It was harsh, but Antonio realized they were devastated, too, and this was their way of coping.

As 1929 wore on, Antonio and Rosa grew closer. They had been friends in Quadri, but their friendship was deepening. Soon they realized they understood each other better than anyone else could. They knew one another's families, they had the same friends, each had known the other's spouse. They shared so much, not just their anguish. Antonio recognized that Margherita's best chance for a good life was in America, not Quadri. Rosa knew it, too. But it wasn't just the concern for the young girl that brought them together. Rosa saw that Antonio was a good and loyal man, a hard worker with many qualities that Giuseppe had.

Giuseppe D'Arcangelo was buried in the D'Amico family plot at Calvary Catholic Cemetery in Pittsburgh. His name is at the bottom of the marker. Giuseppe was Nicholas D'Amico's godfather (the exact family connection is unknown). The American flag has been placed by Giuseppe D'Arcangelo's family in honor of his WWI service.

In October 1929, after a brief courtship, Antonio and Rosa were married.

Some of the neighbors spread rumors about Antonio and Rosa's brief courtship and marriage, but others understood and supported them. None of it mattered to the newlyweds. Their losses had deepened their understanding of life. They kept to themselves, grateful for one another and all that they had.

Antonio now had the opportunity to be the father he wasn't given the chance to be. He understood that he wasn't Margherita's biological father, but Giuseppe was his cousin and best friend, and he was determined to do right by him. He never raised his voice to either Rosa or Margherita. Antonio purchased a radio, and they enjoyed listening to serials and the news. His friends visited once a week to play cards, just like Giuseppe's had.

Rosa continued her routine and learned to bake and cook a variety of delicacies in her gas oven, including lemon meringue pie and gingerbread. She took pride in her ability to master almost any recipe. Of course, she always made favorites that she had learned from her mother: biscotti and pizzelle made with anise.

Antonio worked steadily in the pipe mill. He was content with his role and didn't aspire to be a foreman like Giuseppe had been. The pay was good, and he had no trouble taking care of his new family.

In 1931, when Margherita was three, Rosa experienced two more significant events in her life. She received a letter from her brother, Vincenzo, telling her that their mother, Domenica, had died. Although they corresponded frequently, Rosa was keenly aware of the distance. She thought of her mother's words, about how her grandchildren would visit her one day, and lamented that it could not be so. Also, the house at 41 Rear Boundary became available. Antonio and Rosa saw it as an upward move, so they packed up Margherita and their small household and transitioned to the home a few doors down. Although they were content at 40 Boundary, the fresh start was appealing. Their neighbors at 42 Boundary were another D'Amico family from Quadri. The head of the household was also named Antonio, which was Anglicized to Tony. Tony and his wife, Carmella, were the parents of a large, jangly brood of children. A common walkway known as Diulus Way separated the tenants. Diulus Way led to a set of stairs, which in turn climbed up, up, up to South Bouquet Street. The children were happy to play on the walkway between the houses, daring one another to venture to the top of the stairs. They never made if far before one of the Boundary Street mothers caught them and warned about the dangers of venturing onto South Bouquet alone. When they weren't playing on the walkway, they played in the streets. There was no traffic to speak of, so it was a safe place for the children, and they were always under watchful eyes.

Antonio, Rosa, and Margherita lived at 41 Rear Boundary (where the dining room chairs are located under the awning). The area next to the house is Diulus Way. The stairs in the right background are a long climb to South Bouquet Street (ninety-nine steps).

Antonio, Rosa, and Margherita moved to this house on South Bouquet, situated at the top of Diulus Way. The lived in the right duplex. The home was torn down in 2013 or 2014. Image capture: May 2008, © 2018 Google.

The Pier Street house were Margherita tried to learn to roller skate on the front porch.

This little house on Boundary became the one that held all of Margherita's fondest childhood memories. She never knew Giuseppe, but Antonio was a good substitute and the only father she ever knew. She called him "Papa," and he affectionately referred to her as *la gaugliona*, a Napoli regional term for "little girl." They made homemade root beer, and Rosa and Margherita often ventured into downtown Pittsburgh, the Hill District, or East Oakland to visit family. They traveled to Bloomfield for festivals at Immaculate Conception and occasionally made the long, sad trip to Calvary Catholic Cemetery to visit Giuseppe's grave.

Although Antonio and Rosa knew some English, they spoke Italian at home, and it was Margherita's first language. She quickly learned some English from her parents and the neighborhood children.

In 1933, Margherita was ready to attend school. Rosa made the decision to send her to the private Catholic school, St. Paul Cathedral Elementary, in Oakland. She intended to stick as closely as she could to the plans she and Giuseppe had made for their child. Giuseppe had saved more than enough for her to afford it, and college was also within reach.

Rosa and Margherita left Immaculate Conception and joined the Oakland church that was home to the school. Margherita attended children's mass, while Antonio and Rosa went to the adult services. They were devout Catholics who found solace in their faith.

Rosa was protective of Margherita; it was to be expected, given Giuseppe's loss. She walked Margherita to school on the first day. A nun asked the child's name, and Rosa replied, "Margaret Angelo." The nun encouraged Rosa to never give up her true name, given that it was her heritage. Rosa agreed, and Margherita was then known as Margaret D'Arcangelo. It seemed a fitting compromise for the young American girl.

Rosa had gradually become "Americanized," too. Friends referred to her as "Rose" and "Rosie." She recalled that Giuseppe became

"Joseph," and he'd shortened D'Arcangelo to "Angelo" following the lead of his brother, Charlie. When her signature was needed on official documents, she proudly signed, "Rose Angelo D'Amico." She knew Giuseppe would've approved.

Margaret enjoyed learning. She was smart, quiet, and kind. Her classmates included the McSwigan twins, whose family owned Kennywood Amusement Park, and Anna Rita Curran, who became her best friend.

While Margaret liked school, the prejudice she faced was, at times, overwhelming. Not only was she Italian and discriminated against because of it, her thrifty parents weren't extravagant. The other children looked down on her for being an immigrant and "poor," since she didn't dress in the latest fashions or have a large wardrobe. The nuns who taught at the school encouraged the division by giving the girls of prominent families preferential treatment.

In 1934, shortly before Margaret began second grade, Rosa once again received sad news from Vincenzo. Their father, Gaetano, had died. Rosa grieved quietly, realizing she had a young daughter to raise. At the time, Antonio and Rosa saw another opportunity to better their circumstances. On South Bouquet Street, at the very top of the stairs off Diulus Way, lived yet another cousin from Quadri. Domenico D'Amico and his wife, Ernestina, lived on one side of a large, newish brick duplex. The other side, house number 385, was empty. Antonio and Rosa moved once again, and the spacious quarters suited them. Best of all, they were still close to their family and friends in the Hollow.

Before the summer was out, Rosa told Margaret they were going to take a short trip to Buffalo, NY, and they would get to see Niagara Falls. Rosa had been planning the trip for a while. Her first cousin, Albericio "Albert" Pacella, and his wife, Mary, lived there, along with many other family members. Albert and Giuseppe were roommates at 15 Boundary Street when both were drafted in 1918. Albert was severely wounded in France, where he served in the American

Expeditionary Forces under General John J. "Black Jack" Pershing. When he returned, his work took him to McKeesport, where he met his future wife, Mary Glass. Albert and Mary moved to Buffalo to be closer to his family. He hadn't been able to attend Giuseppe's funeral due to his health, and Rosa wanted to see him. Rosa and Mary corresponded regularly and made plans. Mary insisted on driving to Pittsburgh to pick her up. She would bring her back, too. Mary knew Rosa had experienced a lot of loss the past five years and thought the change in scenery might do her good. Rosa talked with Antonio about it, and he agreed.

Rosa borrowed a few pieces of luggage and packed. Margherita could barely contain her excitement. She'd seen Panther Hollow Lake and each of Pittsburgh's famous three rivers, but she had never seen a waterfall. Rosa and Antonio liked to tell her about *La Cascada*, the waterfall just outside of Quadri that was more than 300 feet high. They promised her that Niagara was higher than that, higher than any of them could imagine.

Mary arrived, driving a large four-door car. Mary and Rosa were progressive women. Mary, who was a first generation American, was the independent type. Few women learned to drive, let alone drive several hundred miles and back again twice. Rosa, whom Giuseppe encouraged to explore her surroundings, was conversant enough in English to ride trolleys around the city and to make transactions at each store she visited. She also did all the grocery shopping; in Italian families, this responsibility traditionally fell to the men. Giuseppe, and now Antonio, placed great faith and trust in her abilities, which built her confidence. Rosa was determined that Margaret would have that same confidence.

The drive to Buffalo was fun and a welcome respite from the daily bustle in the Hollow. Mary and Rosa talked endlessly, and Mary quizzed her about their family in Italy. Mary related stories Albericio had told her about Giuseppe from when they had boarded together at 15 Boundary Street before they were drafted.

Buffalo was a whirlwind for Rosa. She caught up with family, and she and Margaret had dinner with different relatives each day they were there. Margaret played with her cousins, Ralph, Victor, and Dorothy, who were close to her in age. As promised, Mary packed up the car, and they drove to Niagara Falls. Margaret was certain it was the most beautiful thing she had ever seen – the largest, too. Rosa was astonished. She was such a long way from Quadri, in so many ways.

Albericio told Rosa about a government program to compensate WWI soldiers (or their heirs); he had received a small sum of money. He felt that Rosa should apply for Margaret. Rosa thought about it and decided to apply while she was in Buffalo rather than upon her return to Pittsburgh. Albericio made a few calls, and the American Legion had the forms delivered. They visited a notary public, filled them out, and completed all the necessary paperwork. Giuseppe had served a total of six months. Margaret was awarded $10 per month for his service. Rosa was finding ways to help keep Margaret's nest egg growing.

When it came time to say goodbye, the Pacellas implored Rosa to move to Buffalo with Margaret and Antonio, but she explained that their lives were established in Pittsburgh. Family came to see them off, and Mary, Rosa, and Margaret made the long drive back to Pittsburgh.

Although the house on South Bouquet was spacious and close to the Hollow, Antonio learned of a newer brick house at 3815 Pier Street, just off South Bouquet, that was available.

"Another step toward where we want to be," he explained to Rosa. She agreed, and they moved in 1936.

One day, Rosa and Margaret walked to the G.C. Murphy in Oakland. The store was filled with all sorts of fun and interesting things, and Margaret liked to explore the toy department. As she and Rosa strolled the aisles, a section of roller skates caught her eye.

"Mama, please buy me a pair."

Rosa smiled.

"No, they are too expensive, and you might get hurt."

"Please, Mama."

This wasn't typical behavior from the little girl. When Rosa said no, she meant it, and Margaret knew it.

"I said no."

They exited the store, and Margaret broke free. Before Rosa could stop her, she ran all the way home. Rosa finally caught up with her. Margaret had locked herself in the bathroom, aware that she'd not only disobeyed her mother, but crossed many of the busiest streets in their neighborhood without an adult to guide her.

"Come out, Margaret."

"No, Mama."

"It's OK. Please come out."

"I don't want to."

"It's all right."

Rosa's voice was soothing and calm. Margaret cracked open the door and stepped out.

Mama was waiting and gave her a spanking.

"You must never, ever do that again!"

Rosa was beside herself. Not only were the streets dangerous, someone could have taken her daughter. Margaret knew she'd done something very wrong, and she never did it again.

Not long after that, Rosa surprised Margaret with a pair of roller skates that she'd so desperately wanted. The little girl sheepishly accepted them and happily skated around the concrete front porch. She was doing well until she lost her balance and fell backwards. Rosa, the ever-watchful mother, panicked when Margaret almost hit her head on the cement railing as she fell. Antonio was horrified. Rosa instructed Margaret to remove the skates, and she immediately returned them to the store.

Margherita at her eighth birthday party in 1935.

Margherita posing for her first communion, circa 1937.

Their time at this house was short. When a nicer house was offered at 3808, just up the street, they jumped at the chance. The house was a little farther from Boundary Street, but it was still in the neighborhood. South Oakland was different from Panther Hollow; it was filled not only with Italian immigrants but also those from other countries. Everyone worked hard and got along well.

The new house had enough space in back for a small garden, so Antonio dutifully planted tomatoes, green beans, garlic, and various types of hot and sweet peppers.

Rosa, Antonio, and Margaret settled into a steady, contented, routine life. Rosa and Antonio, who had experienced so much grief in the 1920s, found little use for disagreements or squabbles as they made their way in the 1930s. They realized that their time together was a blessing, a true miracle of a second chance. It deepened their faith in God and in one another. They pinned their hopes and dreams on Margaret, and they poured their love into her. She was a gentle and sweet little girl, with deep empathy for others. She would have the better life they all believed they would find when they had made the decision to emigrate to America. Margaret would be someone who didn't have to work as hard as they did; she'd be independent and would know a good man when she found him. They would have grandchildren, whom they would teach to crochet and bake and garden. Rosa and Antonio would tell them about Giuseppe and Quadri. Their grandchildren would learn to love Italy as much as Rosa and Antonio loved America.

As their circle of friends widened, Antonio and Rosa discovered more family that had chosen to settle in Pittsburgh. Many were from Pizzoferrato. One of Rosa's distant cousins, Giulia, and Giulia's husband, Sabatino, were Margaret's godparents. Elena was Margaret's confirmation sponsor. All had ancestral roots in Quadri.

Margaret was far from a spoiled daughter, but her parents indulged her occasionally. She saw the movie poster for *Rosalie*, an Eleanor

Powell vehicle that was released in 1937, and pestered her mother about it.

"Mama, please take me. I want to see it."

"You do? What is it about?"

"I don't know. She dances."

Rosa smiled. Margaret loved Shirley Temple movies, with all the singing and dancing.

"We'll see.

That Saturday, Rosa instructed Margaret to dress in her nicest outfit.

"Where are we going, Mama?"

"I have to get some shopping done. Don't be long."

Margaret dressed quickly, and Rosa took her by the hand. She was disappointed, but knew that if she behaved Mama might buy her a root beer – it cost an entire nickel and came in a big glass. But instead of catching the trolley downtown, Mama turned and directed her toward Schenley Park. Margaret could barely contain her excitement. They were walking toward the Schenley Theater!

"Mama, are we going to see *Rosalie*?"

"Yes, we are. Now, I want you to be on your best behavior and enjoy the movie."

"I will!"

Margaret was enchanted with Eleanor Powell's dancing. Rosa found the film amusing, and she liked the singing and dancing almost as much as her daughter did.

As they walked home, Rosa felt joyful. Although she understood that life wasn't like a movie, she wondered if all the tragedy she'd experienced in America might finally be behind her.

5. A Disrupted Childhood

In early 1939, Rosa began to feel unusually tired. She attributed it at first to a cold and then to the challenge of keeping up with an active child. But when she noticed blood in her urine and began feeling a terrible pain her abdomen, she knew something wasn't right. She confided in Antonio, and he insisted that she see a doctor at once.

It was April; Rosa was in her late forties. She made an appointment with her doctor, whose office was in Pittsburgh Hospital. She tried not to think too much about what could be wrong. But for some reason, she had a bad feeling.

A week later, she saw her doctor. He examined her and then explained that she needed some X-rays.

"Mrs. D'Amico, I believe there's a mass."

"A mass? What does this mean?"

"A tumor. I'm sorry, but I think it's cancer. *Cancro.* You know this word?"

"*Sì,*" she replied in Italian, shocked at what he was saying. "Yes. Yes. Is it bad?"

"We'll see what the X-rays say. Go have them now, and then come back to my office. I'll call Mr. D'Amico."

"He's at the mill. He's working."

"It's OK. I want him here. Do you know where to get the X-rays? The X-ray lab is in the basement. I'll have one of my assistants escort you."

Rosa felt as though she were dreaming. The assistant took her to the lab and then returned to her job. Rosa changed into a robe, did as the technician told her, and then made her way back upstairs to wait for Antonio and the X-ray results.

Antonio arrived about forty-five minutes later.

"Rosa, I came as quickly as I could."

"The doctor says—"

"I know. Let's not get ahead of him. We'll see what he says."

Rosa nodded silently, but her heart sank. She knew that cancer, regardless of how far it had progressed, was usually a fatal diagnosis Was it the stress of being separated from Giuseppe for ten years, and his subsequent death after their brief but meaningful reunion, that caused this? She thought about her stillborn child, about her mother and father and how their deaths came so soon after Giuseppe's. She'd lost so much in such a short time. Most of all, she thought about Margaret. She had to be healthy for her; she just had to be. Perhaps the doctor made a mistake. What if he hadn't? What would happen to her child?

She grasped Antonio's hand, panic-stricken and unable to articulate all that she felt. He was ashen, knowing full-well that the doctor wouldn't have asked him to come from the mill unless he thought it was something serious.

After another hour, the doctor called them into his office.

"We had to wait for the lab to process the X-rays. I asked them to rush them, so they did them as quickly as they could."

The doctor took a deep breath. "See this bright area on the film?" He pointed to a section of Rosa's abdomen on the X-ray. "I'm sorry, Mrs. D'Amico. That's a cancerous mass that has overtaken your uterus. I can see by its size that it's been growing for a while, perhaps years. There's nothing we can do for you now because of how advanced it is. The best that I can tell you is that you may have six months to a year left to live."

He turned to Antonio. "Mr. D'Amico, do you understand what I'm saying? There isn't much time left. I'm so sorry to have to tell you this."

Antonio nodded grimly. Rosa was too stunned to speak. The doctor handed a prescription to him. "To help with the pain," he said. "We'll discuss morphine later. Here's a card with the information for the follow-up appointment."

Antonio took the appointment card and promised the doctor they'd return.

Rosa and Antonio left the doctor's office and walked slowly to the trolley stop.

"Thank goodness Margaret's in school today," Rosa said weakly. "I couldn't bear to explain this to her yet."

Antonio wrapped his arm around Rosa's waist and pulled her close as they waited for their ride and then made the slow walk to their house on Pier Street. They sat quietly in their kitchen, just as they had countless times before.

"I'll make you some tea, Rosie." Antonio stood and put on the kettle

"I don't know how I'm going to tell Margaret."

"Maybe you shouldn't."

"Oh, no. I need to prepare her."

"Just give it some thought."

"Tonio," Rosa said, "what will happen to her? Where will she go?"

Antonio knew Rosa would ask him this, but he couldn't answer her. Although he loved Margaret as though she were his own, he wasn't her biological father. His heart was heavy, almost as heavy as it had been when he had to give up his own daughter thirteen years earlier in 1926. He thought of her often, and wondered how alike she and Margaret might be. They were close in age; if he and Rosa hadn't lost their spouses, the girls would've played together, perhaps even been best friends. He felt devastated by the tragic irony of it all.

"Antonio, is everything all right?"

Antonio was so lost in thought, he didn't hear the kettle whistling.

"Yes, yes. Let me get you your tea." As he poured her a cup, he finally managed to find the words.

"I don't think they'll let Margaret stay with me, Rosa. I want her to, I really do. I don't know how I'd manage it. You know that I couldn't keep my daughter because I was widowed and working in the mill. I'm so sorry."

Antonio's voice trailed off, and Rosa understood that they would have to find another solution.

"Margaret will be home from school soon," she said.

"Yes. We'll talk tonight, after she falls asleep. Maybe we can talk more with the doctor."

"Perhaps the lawyer will have some advice. I have to think about Giuseppe's estate, too."

"Yes. Don't concern yourself with all of that right now. Drink your tea. It will help."

Rosa knew she was blessed to have married two kind and decent men. Her heart ached for Antonio. He'd lost his first wife and his child. Now he was about to lose his second wife and another child. There was no way to make sense of the things that were happening.

Margaret soon arrived home from school, happy to discuss her day while she ate some homemade gingerbread and drank a glass of milk. Rosa watched her carefully, wondering what would happen to her, if Margaret would remember her and what her future might be like. In that moment, she realized she needed to make sure Margaret was going to live with good people.

Antonio and Rosa later discussed what they would tell Margaret, and they decided they wouldn't tell her anything. She was only eleven years old. They'd shielded her from adult concerns, and this wouldn't be any different. They also agreed they would only tell a few close friends about Rosa's condition.

Elena was Margaret's confirmation sponsor and one of Giuseppe's cousins. She lived in a large, three-story house on Parker Street with her husband, parents, sister, and two of her own children. She dropped by the house on Pier Street frequently, often uninvited, and showered Margaret with affection. Antonio thought the affection was an act, and he was leery of her. He'd heard talk in Oakland about the way she manipulated vulnerable people and conned them out of money. Although he was a simple man who minded his own business, his instincts told him to keep up his guard.

"Something about her isn't right, Rosa," he'd say after Elena's visits. "I knew her family in Quadri. Her grandfather was from Pizzoferrato. They weren't good people, and everyone in both villages avoided them. She knows about Giuseppe's estate. That's why she comes around."

But Rosa dismissed Antonio's concerns as a lack of understanding of American culture.

"It's just the way people are in America," Rosa said. "She means no harm. She loves Margaret so much. She gave her an expensive watch, didn't she? What could she possibly gain by doing that?"

It was true; Elena had given Margaret a wristwatch for her confirmation, an almost unheard-of luxury. She even had the back engraved: "Margaret D'Arcangelo." To top it off, Elena attended the party Rosa had hosted for Margaret's eighth birthday. Elena not only brought Margaret a store-wrapped gift, but she fussed over her. It was a sure sign of her affection for the child. Rosa enjoyed watching Margaret soak up the attention, and she aspired to adapt to American culture like Elena had.

Rosa was in awe of Elena and trusted her, but not only because of the family connections. Elena helped families in the neighborhood who had legal questions; one of her cousins was a notary public who worked for an Italian attorney. Elena was savvy enough to direct clients to the attorney, who in turn paid her a finder's fee. Somehow, Elena managed to have herself named as the executrix of a few elderly residents' estates.

"They don't have any family," Elena had said. "It takes up quite a bit of my time, but someone has to do it. The final bills need to be paid, and if anyone owes the estate anything, I make sure it's paid. It's important that their last wishes are carried out, too."

Antonio was at work one day when Elena stopped in.

"I've heard the news, Rosa. I'm so sorry."

She shook her head and grasped Rosa's hand, tears welling in her eyes.

"This is what God wants for me," Rosa said, "so I must accept it."

Elena sat in one of the kitchen chairs, making herself at home.

"Have you made a will?"

"Not yet. I know that I must. Antonio and I will do it."

"You can do it yourself. That's how it works in America. It's not the same as it is in Italy. Your husband doesn't have to be present. Did you know that?"

Rosa shook her head.

"Let me know if you'd like me to help," Elena said. "Margaret's like a daughter to me. You won't be charged anything. I'll take care of everything. You don't need the stress."

Rosa gratefully agreed. She just wanted to spend as much time as she could with her daughter.

"What should I do?"

A small smile flashed on Elena's face.

"I'll call the attorney. He'll write your will in Italian, and my sister will translate it into English for the court. That way, you can understand everything that's being done. The attorney will file it with the court, and the executor will have to make sure everything is done the way you want it to be done."

Elena leaned over in her chair. "Giuseppe's estate could be managed by the executor. Wouldn't that be wonderful? The money could be used however you wanted it to be."

Rosa recalled the plans she and Giuseppe had made to send Margaret to college. She would get to be a teacher after all.

"OK, Elena. Bring the attorney when you can."

"We'll come tomorrow, during the day. Remember, Antonio doesn't have to be here. He's working the daylight shift, right?"

Rosa nodded.

"Yes, no need for him to miss a day of work for this. We can wrap it up very quickly."

Rosa felt relieved, and she wondered why Antonio had been so worried about Elena. The attorney was going to come to her and make sure her plans for Margaret were included in the will. This is the way things were done in America. Antonio was worried for nothing.

When Antonio came home that evening, Rosa didn't tell him about Elena's visit.

The next day, a few minutes after Antonio had left for the 8:00 a.m. shift, there was a knock at the door. When Rosa opened it, she was surprised to find Elena and a sharply dressed gentleman standing on her porch. Rosa invited them in, and Elena explained that the attorney, Mr. Stanicato, was going to help Rosa with her will. Mr. Stanicato shook Rosa's hand and offered his condolences in Italian, and then he pulled some papers out of his breast pocket.

"I took the liberty of drawing up the papers. They're standard."

"Yes, they are," Elena said. She didn't have any formal legal education, but she wasn't going to let that detail stop her.

"I spoke with Elena," Mr. Stanicato said "I think it's best if she's the executrix of your estate. Do you know what that is?"

Rosa nodded yes. "That's the person who makes sure that the will is followed. My first husband died, so I know. He didn't have a will. The court is overseeing the estate. If anything happens to me, it goes to Margaret. It will go to Margaret…"

All she had to do was sign, but Rosa remembered that Giuseppe had told her to read first before signing any piece of paper.

Rosa asked for their patience and began reading. It was in Italian, so she was able to read it, but most of it was over her head. After a few moments, she asked Mr. Stanicato why Antonio wasn't mentioned in the document.

"I'm sorry, Mrs. D'Amico. Is there a reason you'd like me to mention him?"

"I want to give him some of the money. I want him to know how much I love him, and how sorry I am that he's going to be alone."

"OK, we can do that. How much is in the estate?"

Rosa hesitated. She kept a close eye on it and watched the interest make it grow. It was substantial. There was also an outstanding debt.

"Well…it's a lot."

Elena and Mr. Stanicato exchanged glances.

"I can go over the bank accounts with you, Rosa," Elena said. "In fact, we can do that today. You don't have any plans, right?"

"No."

"Good. I know that Giulia and Sabatino owe you money, too. That will add more to the estate."

Rosa caught herself. Elena knew about the loan. Then Rosa remembered that Giuseppe and Sabatino had drawn up the papers at Mr. Stanicato's office. Giuseppe loaned them $1,100 to purchase their home on Boundary. They had fallen on hard times and made some bad property purchases. They had children, and Giuseppe was concerned they might end up homeless. Sabatino said he would pay it back. But Giuseppe died, and Sabatino conveniently forgot about the loan. Rosa pressed the issue whenever she saw Giulia, and their relationship suffered. Even Margaret noticed the change in her mother's demeanor when her godmother appeared, although she didn't know why. Rosa's insistence on repayment had become more forceful in the weeks since her diagnosis. She wanted the estate to be whole again, for Margaret.

"Yes, they owe it to Giuseppe."

"We'll get it sorted out."

Rosa felt a strange mix of relief and dread. If Elena knew about their affairs, who else did? She was embarrassed by her failure to hold Sabatino to his end of the bargain. At least Elena would work with the lawyer to make sure it was paid back. Even if it weren't, there was more than enough for Margaret to finish private school and to go to a good college. Perhaps she would attend the University of Pittsburgh. Their Cathedral of Learning towered over Oakland, an ever-present reminder of the importance of education. Rosa was awed and inspired by its magnificence. In 1926, the residents of Panther Hollow watched as the Indiana limestone used for its exterior was brought in by train on the tracks across from Boundary and hauled up to the foundation. The Cathedral was completed in 1936. Giuseppe was impressed by what he had heard about it, but he never got to see it completed. Rosa did, and she dreamed that one day her daughter might attend classes inside.

After Mr. Stanicato left, Elena made herself at home. She brewed some coffee, and she and Rosa went over the savings accounts. The Orphan's Court of Allegheny County administered the estate, so while Rosa had some leeway, she was careful with the accounts.

Elena explained that Mr. Stanicato wouldn't have to draw up any papers for Sabatino and Giulia.

"They'll return the money once I talk with them."

Rosa didn't understand what Elena meant, but Elena distracted her, so she never gave it another thought.

A few days later, Elena returned with more papers. Rosa had been to the bank and sorted out how much the estate was worth: $5,000. A fortune in 1939. Including the $1,100 owed and a $500 life insurance policy for Rosa, it amounted to nearly $100,000 in today's dollars.

"Frank – I mean, Mr. Stanicato – just needs to know how much you want to leave Antonio," Elena said. "It doesn't have to be much. I think one-hundred dollars will do."

Rosa was aghast.

"I've known him my entire life. We've been married for ten years. I want him to have two thousand dollars. There's still enough for Margaret's schooling and college."

Elena looked pale.

"I think it's too much, Rosa."

"I don't think it is. Two thousand."

Elena stared at Rosa, searching for what to say. Finally, she relented.

"OK. I'll tell him that it's two thousand. In the meantime, read these papers. This is what the rest of the will says. If you agree with it, Mr. Stanicato will bring them to you this afternoon to sign. Then they'll be notarized."

Rosa read carefully. The contents of the house would go to Antonio; her wedding ring, from Giuseppe, was Margaret's. Margaret was to receive most of Giuseppe and Rosa's estate, which would be maintained and managed by the bank under the guidance of the Orphan's Court. Monies would be released occasionally for Margaret's care, until she was no longer a minor. Then, she'd receive the full balance of what remained. This was standard procedure for an orphaned minor who had an inheritance. Not one dime of the estate could be touched without approval. The line of succession was also established. If Margaret died, the estate would go to Antonio. If he passed, Elena, as the executrix, would be the beneficiary.

Elena watched anxiously, trying to gauge Rosa's reaction. Finally, Rosa nodded.

"OK, Elena. I'll sign this. I don't think there's anything else to add."

In April 1939, Rosa signed her will. She tried her best to focus on Margaret, but she was getting sicker. The doctor gave her medicines to ease her queasy stomach, but the pain was growing worse. She was also tired, more tired than she ever remembered being. By October 21, she was confined to a bed in the living room in the home on Pier Street.

"Papa, what's wrong with Mama?"

"Don't worry, little girl. You want to go outside and play?"

"I think I'll stay inside and play with my tea set."

"OK. You be a good girl. Don't be too loud."

Margaret amused herself with her tea set, while Antonio took a cup of tea to Rosa. Some of the neighbors stopped in and made their way into the living room to chat with her. The Bucci family, who lived across the street, was particularly attentive, bringing chicken soup not only for Rosa but for Antonio and Margaret, too.

November 1 was Margaret's birthday. Antonio took her hand and guided her to Rosa's bedside. Rosa, weakened and in agony, smiled at her. She couldn't talk, overcome with emotion and knowing that Margaret couldn't understand what was happening. She thought about Giuseppe, how proud he would have been of their beautiful little girl.

A week later, the pain had become unbearable. The doctor made a house call but couldn't do anything for her. He administered morphine, but as it wore off, Rosa's screams could be heard throughout the neighborhood.

Margaret knew something was very wrong.

"Papa...."

"It's OK, little girl. You can go to bed if you want."

The front of the Pier Street house where Rosa died.
The family occupied both floors of the right apartment, next to Ermine Way.

Rosa's grave at Calvary Catholic Cemetery, Pittsburgh.

Antonio's heart broke, not only for Rosa, but for Margaret, too.

"Are you sure, Papa?"

Margaret's eyes were wide, horrified by her mother's screams. She'd remember the sound the rest of her life.

"*Sì*, yes. It's OK. Go."

Margaret made her way upstairs and crawled into bed. She buried her head into her pillow to drown out her mother's screams.

At 1:30 a.m., on November 8, Rosa died. In the morning, Margaret knew by the silence that something was dreadfully wrong. Antonio's face was drawn and pale, and he barely spoke.

Mrs. Bucci came over, packed a few of her things, and took her to her house.

"You're going to stay with us tonight, Margaret."

"OK."

The little girl didn't argue. Intuitively, she knew that she had to go. Margaret was an obedient child who was taught to respect adults. She desperately wanted to see her Mama. Maybe she was sleeping now, after having such a bad night. Margaret played with the Bucci children. Pittsburgh was cold in November, so they didn't leave the house.

The next day, Mrs. Bucci helped Margaret dress in her best clothes. They chatted, about nothing memorable. Mrs. Bucci took her by the hand, and they walked across the street.

"I'm sorry, Margaret. Your Mama was a good person. You'll be like her when you grow up."

Margaret said thank you, but she still didn't comprehend what was happening. Mrs. Bucci let go of her hand, and Margaret ran up the steps to her house. She pushed open the front door. The house was dark and a little eerie. Her eyes focused; she noticed Papa and some of his friends.

Something was in the living room: a big box with a lid. A man whom she didn't know picked her up so that she could see inside the box.

"Mama! Mama!"

Margaret began crying. She knew Giuseppe had died, and she'd learned from the nuns about how Jesus had died, but she never fully understood what it meant. In that instant, she was hit fully by the realization that she would never see Mama again.

"*Bacia tua mamma,*" the stranger told her. "Kiss your Mama."

The stranger leaned her down toward the casket. She was forced to kiss her deceased mother goodbye. While an Italian custom, it was terrifying for a child who'd never experienced death.

Antonio purchased three plots at Calvary Cemetery, for Rosa, Margaret, and himself. Eventually, he would have a gravestone placed, too.

Margaret was inconsolable. The day of the funeral, the grief-stricken little girl was sent to Elena's house. Elena showed her the bedroom where she'd be staying. It was clean and neat with a large bed.

"Your mother tried to get your Uncle Charlie to come for you, but he didn't respond to her letters or telegrams," Elena said. "She begged me to take you. Don't cause me any problems. Go to school, don't roam around the house, and come for dinner when I tell you."

Margaret nodded in wide-eyed amazement as Elena stormed out of the bedroom. Gone was the fun-loving, affectionate confirmation sponsor she'd known her entire life. She didn't know what to make of this new version of Elena, so in that instant, she decided it was best to steer clear of her and cause as little fuss as possible. She threw herself on the bed and then buried her head in the pillow and cried. She missed Mama. Where was Papa? Was it true about Uncle Charlie? Why was everyone she loved gone?

6. Papa to the Rescue

Margaret slept and slept. The next morning, she awoke to Elena calling for her.

"Margaret! Hurry or you'll be late for school."

Margaret hurriedly dressed and then crept down the stairs.

"You don't have time for breakfast since you're walking. Do you know which way to go?"

Margaret shook her head, so Elena grabbed her by the shoulders and marched her out the door.

Elena pointed. "There's the Cathedral. Walk toward it. You'll cross the Boulevard of the Allies. I guess you know how to use a crosswalk."

Elena turned and slammed the door. Margaret ran down Parker Street, keeping her eyes on the Cathedral. She had been to Elena's house many times before, but her mother always walked her there. Now, she was on her own.

She managed to safely cross the Boulevard, and then she ran as quickly as she could down Bates Street. She stopped as she approached Ermine Way, the alley next to her house on Pier Street. She hesitated before turning into the alley.

To her surprise, Papa was sitting on the back steps.

"Good morning, little girl. I thought you might come this way. How are you?"

Antonio asked the question so genuinely that Margaret started crying.

"I don't want to stay with Elena, Papa. Why can't I stay with you? I miss Mama."

Antonio stood and put his arm around Margaret.

"I'm not allowed," he said. "If you were my little girl…"

"I *am* your little girl," Margaret cried.

"You are really Giuseppe's little girl. We must accept this."

"But you're my Papa."

"Someday it will be better. For now, we must do the best we can. You stop crying now. The other kids are walking to school. You go with them, OK?"

"OK, Papa."

"I'll be here when you walk back. I look for you."

"All right, Papa."

Sniffling and wiping her tears, Margaret started toward Pier Street. She turned back to see Papa watching her. She was comforted to know she would see him again later that day.

She met up with other children from South Oakland and Panther Hollow who were on their way to St. Paul Cathedral Elementary. They always walked together. Now, to join them, she had to walk down South Bouquet, then part of the way down Joncaire Street. The group would climb up a little hill that led to a path in Schenley Park, behind Forbes Field. Eventually, they'd cross Schenley Drive, behind the Carnegie Museum. The children took a shortcut through the museum, which was especially nice in the wintertime since they could spend a few minutes there warming up. Finally, they exited the museum to Forbes Avenue, walked to South Craig Street, at last reaching their destination on North Craig.

Not only had Margaret moved to another part of the neighborhood, the time it took her to walk to school was doubled since she had to make her way from Parker Street. What had been a fifteen-minute walk now took around forty minutes – if she ran part of the way.

That day, the nuns didn't acknowledge her mother's death nor treat her any differently than they always had. It was as though nothing had happened. Margaret secretly hoped that if she walked to the house on Pier, she would find that it had all been in her imagination. Mama would be waiting for her, the house smelling of gingerbread.

When school finished, she walked home. As she approached Pier Street, she held her breath. Margaret turned the corner onto Ermine Way to see Papa sitting on the back steps.

"See, little girl, I told you I'd be here waiting for you."

"Hi, Papa."

"You do good in school today?"

"I tried."

Margaret hung her head. Antonio comforted her the best he could.

"You come by every day you go to school."

"I will Papa."

"You'd better go now. Elena will be worried about you."

"Yes, Papa. Bye."

"Ciao, little girl."

Margaret turned and walked toward Parker Street, but she knew Elena didn't care if she returned. The sad child realized she had nowhere else to go, so she went to Elena's house, straight to her bedroom, and closed the door. She laid down on the bed and wept, burdened under the weight of a heavy sadness that she wasn't sure she could overcome. There wasn't anyone to console her like Mama would have. The loneliness was overwhelming, and she cried herself to sleep.

The next morning, Elena yelled for her again. Margaret felt a gnawing in her stomach. She worked up the courage to tell Elena that she was hungry.

"You slept in," Elena said "I don't have time to fix anything for you now. Rosa might have spoiled you, but I won't. Get going or you'll be late."

Margaret hadn't bathed nor changed nor brushed her hair, yet she was out the door. Elena seemed gleeful to get her out of the house.

True to his word, Papa was waiting for her. When he saw her, he appeared startled.

"Wait a minute, little girl."

Antonio went into the house. When he came back out, he had a biscotti for Margaret.

"Thank you, Papa."

"*Sì*. Hurry now, you walk with the other children."

After a few weeks, Margaret became acclimated to her new routine. Elena wasn't any help, but she occasionally called her down to the dining room for a meal. Elena's mother, Ana, was especially mean. Elena's father, Michele, was much nicer. Once, he ladled some extra soup into her bowl, and Ana yelled at him. Margaret kept her head down, eating as quickly as she could. Ana was furious, and commented that Margaret wasn't to get any extra food. Elena didn't assist Margaret at all, but the little girl was careful to bathe and take pride in her appearance, as Rosa had taught her.

Before long, school was out, and summer was in the air. Margaret made the walk to Pier Street daily, even though she knew that Papa was working shifts. If he was at work or sleeping, she played with the children she knew. Mush ball was a favorite pastime. The large, soft ball was easy to catch and couldn't be hit very far. When they tired of that, the neighborhood children would try and sneak into Forbes Field or peek through the fence and watch some of the baseball games. Elena wasn't keeping track of her, so she spent her days as she pleased.

One evening, Ana dished out Margaret's usual meager supper. Margaret was never allowed to serve herself, as she had done at home. When Margaret had finished eating, Elena told her to go outside and to not come back in until she was called. Margaret sat on the front stoop, listening to the clatter in the kitchen. A while later, Elena called her back inside. Something nudged Margaret to look in the kitchen garbage can. She removed the lid and found a pile of watermelon rinds. Apparently, the family had it for dessert, without her.

Margaret went to her bedroom and cried. She wasn't getting enough food, although there seemed to be plenty in the house. A few days later, she overheard Ana bragging about how Michele's employer had given them the fruit as a gift.

When it came time to start school again, Margaret wondered about her clothes. The ones she had were threadbare from constant use. She asked Elena if she could have a new dress, but Elena scoffed.

"I'm not spending money on clothes for you."

"But mine are worn out, and I'm taller…"

"I said no."

Thankfully, Mama had bought her a new winter coat the previous year. Margaret often looked at it as it hanged in her closet, remembering how happy she was to receive it.

Margaret was embarrassed about her school clothes and still grieved the loss of her mother, but it didn't affect her grades. She was a good student and loved to learn. Margaret was excited to find that her class was going to take a field trip to the Buhl Planetarium, on the city's North Side. She'd been all over the Pittsburgh with Rosa, but never that far. The nuns packed the entire class into cars driven by some of the children's parents for the twenty-minute ride.

The class was fascinated by the display of planets and stars, and they learned a lot about the movement of the planets and their positions in the sky.

As soon as the trip was over, the nuns announced that their rides were waiting. Margaret stepped outside to her classmates piling into cars. Some of the families had limos and asked the nuns to ride with them. No one asked the little girl to join them, and others laughed when she asked if she could ride with them back to Oakland.

Margaret had never been in this part of town, so she didn't know how to get to Parker Street. She began walking, hoping to get her bearings and find her way. After quite a distance, she stopped a man and asked him how to get to Oakland. He was surprised.

"Young lady, you've got quite a way to go – and you're walking in the wrong direction."

He pointed to the general direction of Oakland and told her to stay on the sidewalk. Margaret began to run. It was getting late. She was afraid that she would get lost again and that it would get too dark to see any familiar landmarks. After walking for many hours, she finally found herself back in Oakland. She was very late; it had indeed gotten dark. Margaret hadn't had supper, and Elena couldn't have cared less about any of it.

Later, when Margaret confided in some of her friends about her experience, they asked her which bridge she'd crossed to get back to Pittsburgh. Margaret was shaken. She had no recollection of crossing a bridge. The trauma, fear, and uncertainty she'd faced over the past year had been too much for her. Perhaps it was a blessing that she couldn't remember how she'd made it across the Allegheny River.

The long walk and year of neglect had taken its toll. October had just begun, a chill was in the air, and she was getting sick. Elena and her family weren't feeding her properly or clothing her, and Margaret was doing her best to care for herself. She was pitifully thin, and she looked like a pauper with her shabby clothes.

One evening after school, Elena noticed Margaret wiping her nose.

"Are you catching a cold?"

"I think so."

"I don't need my kids getting sick. Gather your things and come with me now."

Margaret grabbed the few belongings she had, and Elena pointed to the hallway.

"Out there, and follow me."

Elena led her to the stairway.

"Go to the third-floor apartment. I don't want to see you in my extra bedroom again. That's where you'll be staying from now on."

Margaret trudged up to the third floor. When she saw the space, she was relieved to be there. It was a private walk-up apartment; Elena hadn't been able to rent it. She'd developed a reputation in the neighborhood for finding creative ways of keeping security deposits, so renters avoided her.

There was a kitchen, a bath, and a small daybed, which suited Margaret. It reminded her of her own bed, the one she'd had on Pier Street.

She managed to attend school for a few more days, but her body finally gave out. In a sickly haze, she made her way back to Parker Street.

The stairs to the third floor were steep and dark, but somehow the little girl willed herself up them. At the top was her bedroom, the only refuge she had from the frightening, lonely life she lived. She was hungry, cold, and tired, and now she was sick. Pittsburgh's harsh winter was setting in. The attic apartment was cavernous and chilly. She had little to eat, and no one ever bothered to check on her. In the solitude, she thought about her mother, even though the memories made her cry. She didn't want to forget anything about Mama: her smile, her voice, the touch of her hand, the many ways she cared for her. She didn't bother undressing and crawled under the covers as the tears began to flow.

Why am I alone, God? Why did my Mama have to die? Why did they take me away from Papa?

Soon, sleep found her. In her feverish dreams, she walked with her mother to church, to the festival, to school. Her hand slipped into Mama's. They journeyed to the Hill District to visit friends. They made the long trek to her father's grave at Calvary Cemetery. Then, inexplicably, they were home. Mama baked gingerbread men and made homemade root beer while Margaret played with her tea set or skipped rope on the sidewalk on Boundary Street – all under Mama's watchful eye.

"*Gualigona. Gualigiona!* Little girl. Little girl! Wake up. Margherita! You wake up now."

Margaret struggled to open her eyes. She was very weak and wanted to sleep, but she recognized the voice, so she forced herself awake.

"Papa?"

"How long you been up here? How long you been sick?"

"I don't know. They don't give me food, Papa. I only have two dresses and they make me walk all the way to St. Paul's to school. I'm scared. Why won't they let me stay with you, Papa?"

Papa was upset. He was a quiet man, never stern, but his face betrayed his concern. For a moment, she wondered if she had done something wrong; then she remembered that he was always kind and never raised his voice to her. She coughed hard and worried that she might be as sick as her real father had been. Mama told her the story many times. He was a foreman at Jones and Laughlin Steel. He worked as many hours as he could. He caught the flu, then pneumonia. He was only thirty-nine years old when he died.

"I get the doctor. You no move."

As Papa left the room, she burrowed under the thin sheets, and a wave of relief swept over her. Whatever was happening, he would fix it. He was the only father she ever knew, and he always treated her as his own.

Elena was supposed to be Margaret's guardian, but she showed no interest in her. Margaret told Elena that she was ill, that there was a heaviness in her chest and her nose was running – and she was tired, so very tired. Elena looked in on her once and promised to make her some tea, then promptly disappeared. Margaret hadn't seen Elena in days.

Margaret dozed off again but soon was awakened by Papa and the doctor. Papa smiled and held her hand. Dr. Murray opened his bag, took her temperature, and listened to her heart and lungs with his stethoscope.

"How old are you, Margaret?" the kindly doctor asked.

"I'm twelve…almost thirteen."

"That's right. I remember when you were born."

The doctor placed his stethoscope back in his bag and turned to Papa.

"She needs to be someplace warmer than this. It's obvious that she hasn't eaten much of anything for quite a while. She was never in this condition before Rosa passed away…thin…pale…generally uncared for. Bronchitis is setting in. She has a fever. It's a good thing you called me. Frankly, Tony, she could have died if you hadn't come."

Papa patted Margaret on the head.

"I no see her for a few days, so I came to check on her. She will be OK?"

"I think so, Tony," the doctor said. "I have some aspirin for her. It'll help with the fever. Feed her hot soup, as hot as she can stand. Give her lots of water, too. Lots of bed rest, OK?"

The doctor looked thoughtfully at Tony for a few moments, then quietly said, "You really need to get her out of here, you know. I can't emphasize it enough. The neglect—"

"I know," Tony said. "I told them downstairs she will be leaving. I already called the lawyer. I go to the judge and tell him!"

"You're a good and decent man, Tony. I'm sorry you've had so much bad luck in your life. You haven't deserved any of it."

Tony smiled grimly and nodded.

The doctor left, and Tony turned to Margaret. "I get the water and you take the aspirin now. I will not leave you tonight. OK, little girl?"

"Yes, Papa. Yes," she sleepily answered, as she drifted off once again.

7. A Different Life

Papa was true to his word, and he checked on Margaret daily. She grew stronger with the hot soup, homemade bread, and strong tea that the doctor prescribed. Before she knew it, she was ready to start school again. The long trek to St. Paul was intimidating, but she longed for her regular routine, which gave her life some normalcy. She never saw Elena, Ana, or Michele after Papa started caring for her, even though it was their house.

During Margaret's recuperation, Antonio had been making plans. He called the lawyer for Rosa's estate and explained how he had found Margaret – sick, starving, cold, and alone. Margaret's caseworker from the Orphan's Court, Mrs. Thomas, was in touch immediately, and she alerted Mr. Stanicato, who in turn alerted Elena. Mr. Stanicato was wise enough to know when he needed to switch sides, so he prepared for the hearing. Even though Elena was Margaret's guardian and treated everyone with disdain and suspicion, she had no control over the court. Antonio knew this and realized that he had to help Margaret.

Margaret had returned to school for only a few days when she was called out of class. Mrs. Thomas greeted her in the principal's office.

"Hello, Margaret. It's nice to see you again."

Mrs. Thomas smiled warmly, putting Margaret at ease.

"Hi, Mrs. Thomas."

Margaret was hopeful that she was there to return her to Papa. There wasn't anyone else for her to stay with.

"Your Papa, Mr. D'Amico, saw Mr. Stanicato. He was your mother's attorney."

"Mama made a will. Papa told me."

"That's right. You're a smart little girl." Mrs. Thomas smiled. "Mr. Stanicato and I asked the judge for a meeting. Mr. D'Amico had some concerns with Elena…."

"She doesn't feed me. I have to stay on the third floor, alone."

Margaret began to panic. What was going to happen to her?

"We're going to fix that," Mrs. Thomas said. "We're going to see the judge. We'll make sure you don't have to stay there."

"Can I live with Papa?"

The girl's eyes welled with tears. She knew the answer before she asked the question.

"I don't think so, but let's see what the judge decides."

Margaret gathered her school books and put on her coat, and she and Mrs. Thomas rode the trolley to the City-County building.

It wasn't strange to be in the heart of the city. Rosa and Margaret had walked everywhere and experienced all they could. Adventure was never far off, and they enjoyed simple pleasures, like people watching and five-cent root beers. Margaret's heart was full of memories.

The courtroom was intimidating. There were many rows filled with people waiting their turn before the judge. Mrs. Thomas pointed at a row, and suddenly Margaret realized that her Uncle Charlie and Aunt Lena were there, sitting with Papa. Uncle Charlie was her father's brother. Even though Giuseppe had died when Margaret was a baby, Uncle Charlie still visited their Panther Hollow home. His favorite time to visit was during baseball season. The Pirates were his team, and he liked to take the short walk up Joncaire Street to Forbes Field to watch the games. Margaret had fond recollections of visiting her aunt and uncle in California, PA, a small town just south of the city. Margaret, her mother, and Papa would ride the train out of Hazelwood, the tracks trailing alongside the Monongahela River, until it reached its destination. They would stay for a few days at a time. Rosa, Papa, and Charlie grew up together in Italy and were lifelong friends, so they always had a lot of reminiscing to do.

As Margaret nestled in beside her uncle, the caseworker approached a table where Mr. Stanicato was seated. They whispered and shuffled papers, and the judge asked them if they were ready.

"Yes, sir," Mr. Stanicato said. "At the recommendation of Mrs. Thomas, the Orphan's Court caseworker, I am here to petition the court to remove the ward, Margaret D'Arcangelo, from her guardian's home. We've prepared the appropriate paperwork."

Mr. Stanicato handed the judge a few papers.

"What's the reason?"

"Neglect, sir. Mr. D'Amico, the child's stepfather, checked on her and found her starving and sick. There are affidavits that describe all of it in detail. And there's a report from Dr. Murray, too. If Mr. D'Amico hadn't checked on her, Dr. Murray says that she would have died. She was malnourished and had bronchitis."

"I see. Give me a few minutes to go over this information."

Margaret fidgeted as the judge read the papers. She didn't understand everything that was being said, but she tried her best to pay attention.

"This is appalling," the judge said. "Mrs. Lupo, what do you have to say about this?"

It was only then that Margaret saw Elena. She was on the other side of the courtroom, sitting with her mother and sister, and stood to talk to the judge.

"They are lying. We are a loving family, and we've treated her like one of our own. We go to mass every Sunday."

"How do you explain her condition, or the doctor's report?"

"She doesn't want to eat. I can't make her bathe."

"She's twelve-years-old. Several witnesses have testified that you left her alone on the third floor of your house."

"It's nice. It's an apartment. There's a small kitchen."

"You left her to fend for herself after her mother died. You're also the executrix of the estate, are you not?"

"Well, yes, I am. And I've brought some papers with me."

"What papers?"

"The estate should make a fair payment to me given that I've taken care of her and provided her with room and board. I took her in because her mother begged me, when she was dying. The girl's own family didn't want her. I did the right thing."

"And what exactly do you think a fair payment is?"

"It's all in these papers."

Elena handed the judge a few sheets of paper. He glanced over them and looked disdainfully at her.

"Margaret," the judge said, "come with me."

Margaret looked at her uncle and Mrs. Thomas. They both nodded at her.

The judge motioned for the stenographer to follow them, and he led them to his chamber.

"Margaret, who is telling the truth?"

Margaret hesitated.

"Please don't be afraid. I want you to be safe and happy."

"Papa and Mrs. Thomas are. Elena never feeds me. My class went on a field trip to the Buhl Planetarium. I had to walk home. No one came to get me."

"You walked from the Buhl Planetarium to South Oakland?"

"I got lost because I went in the wrong direction, but I asked a man, and he told me which way I had to go."

The judge and Mrs. Thomas looked at each other.

"Please let me stay with Papa. He takes care of me. I miss him."

Margaret began crying.

"Don't worry, little girl," the judge said. "I might not be able to let you stay with Papa, but you have family here today."

"Uncle Charlie and Aunt Lena," she said tearfully.

"We'll see what we can do, OK?"

Margaret nodded, and Mrs. Thomas gave her a handkerchief to dry her tears.

The three left the chamber and went back into the courtroom.

"Now, where was I?"

The judge shuffled the papers Elena had given him.

"Am I reading this correctly? What is the amount you're asking, Mrs. Lupo?"

"I think a hundred dollars a month is fair. I had her for ten months. That's almost a year!"

The judge looked at Margaret and smiled, then he glared at Elena.

"I grant Elena Lupo ten dollars per month for ten months, for a total of one-hundred dollars, for room and board for Margaret D'Arcangelo, ward of the court."

Margaret watched as Elena's facial expression turned from smugness to anger. Her mother grabbed her arm.

"Your honor…"

The judge's displeasure was evident. Elena stopped talking and sat down, but her anger was tangible. It was a memory that would stay with Margaret for the rest of her life.

"Mr. and Mrs. Angelo, thank you for coming today," the judge said. "I'm grateful that Mr. D'Amico contacted you. If you agree, I'm going to grant you custody of Margaret. This poor child has been pitifully neglected – little food, few clothes. Given that her mother took the time to make a will and planned for strict oversight of her very substantial estate, she never intended for this to happen to her daughter. She believed Margaret would be in good hands. I'm sorry to say that she trusted the wrong person. Now, I'm going to trust you. Margaret is your niece, your family. Don't let me down. The bank that manages the trust will continue to do so. Any requests for expenditures must come through this court, and I assure you that I'll grant them if they're reasonable. Mrs. Thomas will continue in her capacity as Margaret's caseworker. Mrs. Thomas, I understand that you've arranged with Mr. and Mrs. Angelo for Margaret to move in with them."

"Yes, your honor. I've been to the house. She has her own room, and they've purchased a new bedroom suite. They're prepared."

"That's wonderful. Margaret, if you ever have any questions or need anything, you are to tell Mrs. Thomas, understand? Whatever you tell her is between the two of you."

"Yes, sir."

"OK. Thank you, and I am hoping for the best for you. Next case!"

In the whirlwind of decisions, Margaret could barely breathe. Her aunt and uncle ushered her into the hallway, where they put on their coats and quietly talked about catching the train.

"Little girl, little girl."

Margaret looked up, and Papa was standing next to her.

"You no worry now. You be OK. You go to California."

Antonio was stammering in his broken English, doing his best to assure the little girl.

"I don't want to go to California, Papa. I want to stay with you."

"The judge no allow."

Margaret began sobbing uncontrollably.

"Margherita, no cry," Uncle Charlie said. "You stay with us. You stayed before."

"I know, Uncle Charlie. But Papa…."

"I see you soon, Margherita. I take the train and visit. OK?"

Margaret saw the pain in Papa's face and understood that it was pointless to try to convince anyone to let her stay with him.

"OK, Papa."

They said their goodbyes as the train pulled in, and soon Margaret, Uncle Charlie, and Aunt Lena were on their way.

The house on High Street in California was, at once, familiar yet foreboding. Margaret wondered about how far she'd have to walk to school, if she would be accepted and, most of all, how soon she might see Papa.

Aunt Lena showed her to her upstairs bedroom. The furniture was new, and Margaret felt hopeful.

Uncle Charlie and Aunt Lena must really want me, she thought, *if they went to all this expense and trouble.*

She opened the closet. Two new dresses were hanging there.

Aunt Lena called her downstairs.

"It's time to eat, Margherita. Come now."

Margaret bounded down the stairs. Uncle Charlie was already seated.

"You sit here, on the side, between us," Aunt Lena said.

Margaret did as she was told, and Aunt Lena placed a large bowl on the table filled with linguini, tossed with red sauce. There was salad and bread, too.

Aunt Lena served Uncle Charlie first, then Margaret, whose eyes widened at the sight. She ate every bite. Although the sauce wasn't very good, she was hungry, so she didn't complain. It was better than anything she'd had at Elena's house.

After they finished, Uncle Charlie went to the basement. It was mid-October. Although there weren't any baseball games, he'd have a beer and find something to listen to on the radio.

Margaret helped Aunt Lena clean the kitchen. She noticed that Uncle Charlie and Aunt Lena weren't exactly attentive, but at least they fed her, and the house was clean and comfortable.

The next morning, Margaret awoke early, washed, and dressed. Lena was waiting for her in the kitchen.

"Here's some toast. School starts at nine. Go to the top of the street and turn right at the stop sign. Keep walking until you see it."

Margaret gulped down the toast and ran out the door as quickly as she could – she was anxious for her first day at her new school. Although she was nervous about meeting new classmates, she longed for the normalcy of her school routine.

On her way out, she nearly ran into another girl who was passing by the house.

"Hey, who are you?" the girl said. "I've never seen you before."

The girl smiled broadly, but Margaret bowed her head and didn't answer.

"What's the matter? Cat got your tongue?" The girl laughed hard and nudged Margaret. "I'm Flora. Everybody calls me 'Sis.' I live over there." She tilted her head at the house right next door to Uncle Charlie's.

"I'm Margaret. I'm from Pittsburgh. I live with my Uncle Charlie and Aunt Lena now."

"You're from Pittsburgh? Wow. That's far away. I'm twelve. How old are you?"

"I'm twelve, too."

"Are you in eighth grade this year?"

"Uh-huh."

"I'm in eighth grade, too. I guess we're friends, Margaret. You want to be friends, don't ya?"

Margaret could hardly believe her ears.

"Yes, I sure do!"

Sis grinned, took Margaret's arm, and walked her to school.

"We're going to Republican School, at the end of Pennsylvania Avenue. I'll walk home for lunch with you, too."

Margaret had always eaten lunch at St. Paul. Coming home for lunch was new for her.

"I'll introduce you to everyone. They're all mostly nice."

Sis helped Margaret find her classes. It helped that they had the same ones.

Margaret's best friend, Flora "Sis" Basilicato Mihalina.
Photo courtesy of the Basilicato-Mihalina Family.

A few weeks later, Margaret returned home from school to discover Mrs. Thomas, her caseworker, sitting in the living room with Aunt Lena.

"Hi, Margaret. How are you?"

"I'm OK."

"I got permission from the judge to drop in and check on you. I hear you're doing well in school."

"Yes, ma'am."

"Your Aunt Lena tells me you like living here, that all of you are happy and get along fine."

Margaret didn't know what to say. She looked at Mrs. Thomas, then at Lena. Then, she slowly nodded.

"Is there anything you want to tell me?"

"No, I don't think so."

"All right, Mrs. Angelo. It appears to me that you and Mr. Angelo are providing a loving home for this child. I won't be back, unless I'm called."

Mrs. Thomas handed a card to Margaret. "This has my phone number on it. If you ever have any questions or need help, you can call me, OK?"

Margaret's heart sank. Something was off, but she didn't know what.

Lena and Mrs. Thomas said their goodbyes. When Mrs. Thomas drove off, Lena turned to Margaret and scowled.

"Horrible woman. I'm glad I'll never see her again. And neither will you."

Margaret wasn't sure what Lena meant, so she went back to her bedroom and did her homework. She always excelled at school, and now it was an escape for her.

And so it went for four or five months. Although life wasn't the same as it had been with Mama and Papa, it was better than it had been with Elena.

Opening her closet before school one morning, Margaret discovered that none of her dresses were there. Perhaps Lena didn't have a chance to put away the laundry. Margaret went to the kitchen to ask about it.

"Aunt Lena, I need a dress for today."

"Go downstairs," Lena said.

Frightened by the tone in her aunt's voice, Margaret ran to the basement. Uncle Charlie had remodeled it, so it wasn't a dark, damp space like some were. She quickly glanced around and saw her clothes heaped in the laundry tub.

"Do your own laundry," Lena yelled from the top of the stairs. "I'm too sick!"

Next to one wall, near the window, was a wringer washer. Mama had told her they were dangerous and warned her never to go near it; she refused to let Margaret even watch her operate it. Now, she was expected to wash clothes. She would have to figure out how to work the machine herself.

Frightened and apprehensive, Margaret decided to put off the task until she returned from school. She chose a dress from the pile and quickly changed so she wouldn't be late for school.

Soon, Margaret wasn't just doing her own laundry; Lena tasked her with washing Uncle Charlie's filthy work clothes from the mine, too. The little girl struggled to get them through the wringer, but she did. Lena, yelling from the top of the stairs, insisted that Margaret scrub

Charlie's long johns and socks on a washboard with yellow soap, since the wringer wouldn't do an adequate job. Margaret did the best she could. She dragged the heavy basket filled with wet clothes outside and hung them out to dry.

She finished the rest of the laundry and then went upstairs. Her hands were raw and bleeding from the soap and washboard. Lena frowned at her.

"Don't forget to take them off the line when they're dry. I don't want them hanging out there all night."

Margaret was too tired to look at Lena, let alone acknowledge her command. She sat at the table, waiting for her uncle. Her mind was working – if she could get him alone for a few minutes, she'd tell him what Lena was doing. She was certain that he wouldn't like it.

One evening, when they finished eating, Aunt Lena directed her to get ready for bed.

"It's been a long day. I'll be up soon to check on you."

Margaret hadn't been in bed long when Aunt Lena stepped into her room.

"Oh, you're in bed already. That's fine." Aunt Lena paused. "Before you leave for school in the morning, you'll scrub down the kitchen ceiling and walls. They'd better be done before you leave, too."

"But I have to go to school."

"I don't care."

Aunt Lena slammed the door, leaving the little girl confused and terrified. Did she do something wrong? Where was Uncle Charlie?

She wept long into the night, not daring to sleep for fear that she wouldn't awaken in time to scrub the walls. When she entered the kitchen the next morning, Lena was waiting for her.

"Make sure the water's hot. You're younger than I am, and I'm sick. Carry it up from the basement yourself and get to work."

Margaret hurriedly changed into one of her old dresses and began, frightened that she wouldn't finish before school started. She had no idea what consequences she'd face if she didn't complete the task. The walls were very dirty because of the coal heat, and the little girl had to scrub as hard as she could. One wall, two walls…she was exhausted and couldn't do anymore. Margaret went to her bedroom and cried. After a while, she washed up and slowly changed for school.

Soon, Lena called her.

"Come down now and get your breakfast, or you'll be late."

Margaret crept down the stairs.

Margaret was concerned about returning home for lunch. She hadn't finished scrubbing the walls, and she considered what her punishment might be. But when she returned home for lunch, Lena acted as though nothing had happened.

"Oh, you're home for lunch? I didn't fix you anything, but there's some milk."

Margaret gulped it down, anxious to leave before they could talk about the walls.

Lena watched her intently. "I never drink milk. In Italy, we give it to the pigs."

Margaret sat quietly, trying not to provoke Lena, and wondering what she meant. Lena always got milk from the milkman. Someone was drinking it. Margaret sensed that she was spoiling for a fight, although she didn't know why. Suddenly, there was a knock on the door.

"Who could that be?"

Margaret leaned over from her seat at the table to see who was at the front door. It was Sis!

"Is Margaret ready to go back to school?"

"I suppose. Margaret!"

Margaret leaped up from the table to join Sis.

"Thanks," Margaret said to Sis. "I was worried she might make me stay home."

"Why would she do that?"

"She wanted me to finish a chore this morning before I left for school, but I didn't."

"Is that all? Do it later. Come on, we have gym class this afternoon."

Margaret couldn't bring herself to tell Sis about how Lena expected her to scrub walls before she left for school. Mama had never asked her to do anything like that.

Strangely, Lena never said anything about the walls again that day. Margaret went to her room and did her homework, avoiding contact with her aunt.

It wasn't long before Margaret and Sis grew to be the closest of friends. Sis had lost her mother, too; the young girls understood each other. Eventually Margaret confided in her about everything that had happened so far in her short life. Sis listened, spellbound. Most importantly, she believed every word Margaret told her. She encouraged Margaret to ignore Lena as much as possible, and she wondered why Uncle Charlie didn't help Margaret. After thinking about it, Margaret wondered, too. He was her uncle, after all – her father's brother.

One bleak Friday evening, not long after she'd move to California, there was a knock at the door. It was Papa! He'd come to visit for a few days. Margaret was overjoyed, and so was he. She remembered the train rides with Papa and Mama to California and how they'd stay with Uncle Charlie. If only Mama was there now.

Saturday was filled with chatter. Papa brought Margaret some of her favorite candies, and she laughed when he told her stories about some of the children in the neighborhood. Lena prepared a nice luncheon tray with mortadella, prosciutto, salami and cheeses. Margaret made herself a sandwich, and Antonio smiled approvingly.

That evening, Antonio hugged her goodnight. Uncle Charlie and Aunt Lena said their goodnights, and the house grew quiet.

Sunday morning, Margaret played on the front porch while the adults talked in the kitchen. The front door slammed, and she looked up to see Papa hurrying down the street as fast as he could, toward the train station.

"Papa! Papa!"

He turned and waved but didn't stop or say a word.

Margaret asked Charlie what was wrong, but he refused to respond.

She knew they had to have thrown Papa out because he wouldn't just leave without a proper goodbye. While she would never learn the reason for Papa's unusual behavior that day, Margaret was beginning to see her aunt and uncle's true natures. But she still couldn't understand what had made them that way.

8. Transitioning

Margaret hadn't seen much of her Uncle Charlie. He worked steadily in the coal mine, and lately he was putting in a lot of double shifts. She needed only a few minutes with him, though. Perhaps she could speak with him over the weekend.

In the meantime, Lena made her life miserable. Margaret fearfully did her bidding, every chore Lena could imagine, and then some. In addition to doing the laundry and dishes, Lena even had her move furniture around. The weary little girl was so exhausted that she caught herself nodding off at supper.

Lena prepared linguini with her awful tomato sauce daily. She purchased the pasta in twenty-pound boxes. Margaret grew to hate it and wished for some protein, like a little of the beef or sausage her mother used to make.

Occasionally, one of the neighbors who knew about Lena's temperament would invite the little girl to dinner. Margaret knew better than to accept. The neighbors would sneak food to her or wrap some baked goods that she could slip into her dress pocket. Margaret kept her handkerchief on top of those treats, hiding them until she made her way to her bedroom, where she could savor every morsel. She was careful not to leave any telltale crumbs for Lena to find.

Margaret believed that Lena was snooping around her bedroom. Although she didn't have much, she had noticed that her dress shoes would be overturned or her bed would be messy, even though she'd made it before she left for school. Margaret began taking great pains to hide her mother's wedding ring, which she'd received upon her death. Sometimes, she wore it to school just to keep track of it. At least

Lena couldn't meddle with the photo of her with her parents, which was taken on her first birthday. The picture was large and hung on Margaret's bedroom wall. She knew that Uncle Charlie had taken the time to put it there for her because Lena wouldn't have tolerated her walls being touched by anyone else.

One evening after supper, when Uncle Charlie made his customary retreat to the basement, Margaret saw her chance.

"I have to wash another load of clothes."

Lena smirked. "It's about time you did something on your own, without me telling you to do it. I don't feel well, and I can't do everything around here. Don't disturb your uncle. He works hard and needs some time to himself."

Rosa's wedding ring.

Margaret nodded and made her way to the basement. There were only two or three items in the basket, so she quickly ran them through the wringer. Lena would be none the wiser; the laundry was getting done, and that was all she cared about.

Margaret as a sophomore and later as a senior at East Pike Run High School.
Her cruel and unstable home life was taking a noticeable toll.

Undated photo of Margaret, Charlie, and Lena in the backyard on High Street in East Pike Run Township (California), PA.

Standing on her tiptoes so that she could see over the washer, Margaret looked out the window. Uncle Charlie was sitting on the back porch with a beer, listening to the radio. She quietly opened the basement door.

"Uncle Charlie?"

He looked at her, crossly.

"I'm sorry, Aunt Lena told me not to bother you, but I have to tell you something. She's making me do all the work. I've scrubbed the floors and walls, washed the windows, washed the dishes and clothes...I'm so tired that I want to sleep in school. Mama never made me do all of this. Please, can't you talk to her?"

The little girl's plea was pathetic and yearning, hoping for an ounce of familial understanding and caring. Instead, Charlie got up without saying a word and went to his garden.

Had he heard what she'd said? He had to have heard. Why didn't he care? The sad little girl, whose grief seemed to know no bounds, discovered that there was even more to bear, and she wept hysterically.

Crushed, she climbed back upstairs, and Lena yelled something at her about the laundry.

Margaret ignored her and walked the flight of stairs to her bedroom, where she cried herself to sleep yet again.

Early the next morning, Margaret developed a plan. Mrs. Thomas told her to call if she needed anything, so she would do just that. Sis' family had a phone, and Margaret knew that she'd let her use it. They'd walk around the block and approach the houses from the other side, to avoid Lena seeing her. Margaret wouldn't risk angering her, especially over this. She had no idea how she'd retaliate. Even if neighbors were courteous to Lena and she reciprocated, as soon as they were out of earshot, she would call them names or mock them. As cruel as Elena was, she'd never done that. Certainly, Rosa never had. Such duplicitousness was a new experience for the child.

Margaret looked in her bottom dresser drawer, where she'd kept Mrs. Thomas' card and her comic books. Occasionally, Mama had given her dimes to purchase one, and she brought her two favorites with her to California – Superman and one about Lou Gehrig. But something was wrong. Mrs. Thomas' card was missing, and so were the comic books. Margaret panicked. Perhaps they were in a different drawer. There were only three, and she didn't have much in any of them, so they would have been easy to spot. Suddenly, it dawned on her: Lena had been snooping. She must have taken the business card and the comic books. That was the only explanation. Margaret sat on the bed, feeling utterly defeated. She'd pinned her hopes on contacting Mrs. Thomas; she'd promised to help. Margaret sobbed as she tried to make sense of her situation.

Maybe there's a reason, she thought to herself. *Where would I go? Nobody wants me, except Papa, and they won't let me live with him. Uncle Charlie and*

Aunt Lena must have wanted me. They bought me this bedroom suite and got the bedroom ready for me. I don't understand, God.

Margaret met Sis outside for their daily walk to school and told her about the business card and the comic books. Sis listened intently and was flabbergasted. Sure, she was a child too, but even she had some privacy.

"Maybe you should tell on her. Maybe the principal."

"He couldn't do anything…could he?"

"I don't know."

The little girls mulled it over but couldn't come up with an answer. Margaret resigned herself to her situation at home.

It was almost November 1, 1941: Margaret's birthday. She would be fourteen-years-old. She was excited about it, but she knew not to expect anything. Lena only cared about her nieces and nephews – she went all-out for their birthdays. When they dropped into visit, Lena always prepared a variety of food for them and gave them twenty-dollar bills. Margaret would watch, bemused, as Lena practically broke her neck running upstairs to get the money out of her cedar chest, where she thought no one could find it. At first, Margaret was amazed. She'd never seen twenty-dollar bills before. Lena acted as though she was careful with money, but she handed over those twenties as if they were nothing.

In the end, all that Margaret could think about was her mother, how she would have fussed over her and made her one of her delicious two-layer yellow cakes with chocolate frosting. If she closed her eyes, she could taste the airy cake and fluffy frosting. Papa usually gave her a quarter, a small fortune. Margaret would walk to the little store at the end of Pier Street with Mama and buy some penny candy, being careful not to spend her entire quarter in one trip. She'd share with Mama and Papa, laughing and discussing which flavors were their favorites. Later, Papa would turn on the radio or play some music on the gramophone, while Margaret sprawled on the living room floor playing with her paper dolls or tea set.

Margaret had done a lot of growing up the past two years. She'd gone from an idyllic, nurturing childhood into a nightmare, and then another nightmare. This situation was worse because those who were entrusted to care for her were family. She often blamed herself; she must have done *something* to cause this. Margaret was learning how vicious people could be. Because she was a child, she couldn't understand that she wasn't to blame, and shouldn't have been subject to such abuse.

One Sunday afternoon, a few days after her birthday, there came a loud knock on the door. Lena opened it to find Charlie's brother Nick and some of his family standing there. Margaret's jaw dropped. She'd only seen her Uncle Nick a time or two before, and he'd been thrilled to see her. He'd asked her about school and her friends, smiling and enjoying the conversation. She wondered if he would be unkind now too, like Uncle Charlie was, but her fears were unfounded.

"Margherita!" he said. "It's wonderful to see my little niece. How are you, sweetheart? Happy birthday!"

Margaret was unable to speak. No one had ever called her "sweetheart" before, and she found it enchanting when spoken with Uncle Nick's Italian accent. He'd wished her a happy birthday – she was beside herself that someone remembered.

"This is your Aunt Carmela, and these are your cousins. That's Elizabeth and her husband Ed. They drove us from Canonsburg so that we could visit." He laughed. "And this is my Ada. Louise, Grace, and Amerigo couldn't come with us today. Maybe next time."

Ada stepped forward and shyly handed Margaret a gift, then another. Margaret looked at Lena, who nodded her head approvingly.

"Thank you."

"Open them!" Ada squealed. She was anxious for Margaret to see the gifts, which included some new handkerchiefs and lingerie. Ada giggled at the lingerie, and Elizabeth rolled her eyes. Margaret didn't have any siblings and watched their interactions with a mixture of envy and awe.

"My daddy brought you some money, too," Ada told Margaret.

Margaret shyly smiled. "Thank you."

"You girls can go outside and play," Lena said. "Don't get your nice clothes dirty."

Margaret smirked at the hypocrisy of Lena's statement. She wasn't wearing her nice clothes, and she knew Lena couldn't have cared less about Ada's.

The cousins ventured outside, while the adults stayed inside and talked. They played tag and ran until they were tuckered out. They amused themselves for hours, getting to know each other and enjoying one of the last nice days of fall.

Then, much to Margaret's surprise, Lena called them in for supper. There was mortadella and prosciutto, cheese, thick slices of bread, and lots of olives. Margaret couldn't believe her eyes. She politely waited for the guests to fill their plates first, as Mama had taught her, then she filled hers. She didn't look, but she knew Lena was staring at her, angry that she'd made two sandwiches. Margaret didn't care.

After they ate, the girls played some more outside. Sis wondered what all the commotion was about, and Margaret introduced her to her cousin. They discussed their favorite school subjects and played together. Margaret sadly wondered why life couldn't be like this all the time.

Before too long, Uncle Nick and Uncle Charlie stepped out on the front porch and shook hands. Aunt Carmela, Elizabeth, and Ed, followed by Lena, came next. They said their goodbyes and got into their car to return to their home in Canonsburg. Margaret watched longingly as the car proceeded up High Street, with Ada waving from the window.

"Come visit us soon, Margaret!" Ada yelled. "We'll be waiting for you!"

For the first time in a long while, Margaret felt wanted and loved. She marveled at the events that had taken place that day. Her happiness was temporary, though.

"Get inside and clean up this mess," Lena said. "You ate enough for two. What is wrong with you? You know better than that. Those horrible people probably think that I don't ever feed you."

Margaret looked at Uncle Charlie, who glowered at her.

"I guess I'll have to go to the store and get some more lunch meat for your bucket," Lena said to him. "They showed up uninvited, and I had to feed them, considering the distance they came. Takes a lot of nerve."

Charlie never said a word, then suddenly stormed off to the basement.

Margaret recalled how Papa had left in a rush, and it slowly dawned on her that her aunt and uncle weren't welcoming or friendly people. When neighbors dropped in, Charlie and Lena didn't have any qualms about telling them to leave. They never visited anyone in the neighborhood, except Lena's family. Perhaps Papa had eaten too much or overstayed his welcome in some way.

She washed and dried the dishes, wiped the table, and mopped the floors. For once, the work didn't seem too bad. Margaret realized that she had family who were *normal* and who genuinely seemed to like and care for her. She was lost in thought, then realized she didn't know how much money Uncle Nick had given her. She decided to ask Lena.

"Aunt Lena, Ada said that Uncle Nick brought me some money."

"What do you need money for? It costs us money for you to stay with us. Do you think all this food and your clothes are free? How about the electricity and water?"

Margaret wasn't surprised. She thought about Lena's nieces and nephews, and she wondered if Uncle Nick had given her a twenty-dollar bill that ended up in Lena's hands. She trudged up to her bedroom and carefully placed the handkerchiefs and new lingerie in her dresser. The drawer looked large because there was so little in it.

At least I don't have to hide these, she thought.

The next morning, Margaret tucked one of her new handkerchiefs into her dress pocket, and she felt special all day. She showed it to Sis, who was pleased that Margaret had indeed received something for her birthday.

And so proceeded the rest of the school year. Margaret did chores before and after school and all weekend long. If there weren't any chores, Lena found ways to create some for her. She ate linguini until she couldn't any longer, so she stopped eating it altogether. Margaret grew very thin, and her hip bones showed. Occasionally, when Lena was out of the house, Margaret cooked herself an egg for a sandwich, but milk sustained her. She looked forward to spring and then summer, when she thought she might be able to get out of the house and away from Lena for a while.

In March, when the weather began to moderate, Lena announced a new task for Margaret.

"We're making a garden, and you're hauling the dirt."

Margaret was surprised; Lena made it sound as though she was a wheelbarrow or a mule.

For weeks, Uncle Charlie filled bags of topsoil on one side of his large garden, then Margaret had to carry or drag them (however she was able) to the other side. Then, Lena commanded her to haul some to the front of the house, about fifty feet up a steep slope.

"My flowers need fresh soil," she said.

Margaret had no choice but to do the backbreaking work; she was terrified of what the consequences might be if she didn't. Although she was fourteen years old, until then, she had led a sheltered life. The trauma of losing her mother, her Papa, and her home had left her broken, defeated, and alone. It was a cruel existence, but it was the only one she knew. Uncle Charlie and Aunt Lena weren't remotely sufficient replacements for her parents, but they were all she had. If she ran away, where would she go, and to whom? How would she get there? She didn't have any money. Lena monitored her mail, both incoming and outgoing. She could write to Uncle Nick but that didn't mean he'd receive the letter, and Lena had forbidden her from writing to Papa, her godmother, or any of her childhood friends from Panther Hollow and Oakland. Lena isolated her, and Margaret was in survival mode.

One day, when Lena was napping, the mailman arrived. Lena had given her strict instructions to never touch the mail, but Margaret's curiosity got the best of her. She was surprised to see a letter addressed to her from her cousin, Victor. Victor lived in Buffalo, and Margaret remembered when she and Rosa had visited them in 1934. When she was old enough to write, she and Victor became pen pals. She was never exactly sure of how they were related, but Mama had referred to the Pacellas as cousins, and that was all she needed to know. Victor was two years older than her, and sometimes Margaret imagined what it would be like to have an older brother like him. She tucked Vic's letter into her pocket and then carefully placed the rest of the mail in the box, where Lena could later find it and be none the wiser.

Late that night, when she was certain that Charlie and Lena were asleep and wouldn't check on her, Margaret quietly opened the letter. She turned on her lamp so that she could read it. Victor asked if she was all right and wondered why she hadn't responded to his letters. At first, Margaret was puzzled, then she grew angry when she realized Lena had been intercepting his correspondence. She considered who else might have written to her. Lena's meddling had gone too far. Margaret might not be able to do much about her situation, but she would find a way around this.

Margaret devised a plan. She'd use paper from school, and she knew where Lena kept the envelopes and stamps. There were plenty of opportunities to "borrow" some, and Lena often lost count of how many stamps she'd used. If Margaret were careful, Lena wouldn't ever miss what she took.

The tricky part would be mailing and receiving letters. For this, she turned to Sis, who helped her best friend every chance she got. Sis told Margaret to write to Victor from their address, using Sis' name on the return address. To make sure they weren't caught, Margaret had her cousin write to her using Sis' name. This way, even the mailman wouldn't know what was taking place, and he wouldn't accidentally drop off a letter addressed to Margaret at Lena's house.

Margaret and Sis were thrilled with their plan. Margaret immediately wrote to her cousin Vic, explaining the situation. Victor was upset to hear about what was happening and agreed to follow her instructions. Soon, Margaret and Vic were corresponding on a regular basis once again. It was a bright ray of hope in her otherwise bleak reality. In her letters to Victor, Margaret divulged how she was treated. He wrote and told her how sorry he was for her, and he asked if she might be able to endure it for just a few more years. Once she was finished with high school, she could leave. Margaret appreciated his advice, but she wasn't sure how much more she could tolerate.

A month later, Margaret was sitting in class when the loudspeaker crackled.

"Pearl Harbor has been bombed by Japan."

Margaret corresponded regularly with her cousins, Victor and Ralph Pascell (Pacella) during WWII. This photo of Victor was taken in Hawaii.

The children looked at one another and then to their teacher, who appeared shaken at first but quickly recovered. He pulled down the large world map and covered the blackboard.

"Here's where Japan is," he said, using his pointer to guide the students. "Here's where Pearl Harbor is. It's in Hawaii. It's one of our largest naval bases."

Soon, men from her neighborhood were being drafted. Boys just a few years older than Margaret quit school and signed up to serve. The school and community kicked into fundraising mode, selling U.S. Savings Bonds to fund the war effort.

Uncle Charlie's patriotism was unquestionable. He attentively followed the war, reading two newspapers a day and tuning into news on the radio. He purchased a large console radio for the living room, so that Lena and Margaret could listen, too. Margaret asked him about his service in WWI, and for once, Charlie responded. He told her that he'd fought in the Battle of the Argonne Forest. He paused, and his eyes widened at the memories. Charlie muttered, "Goddamn. *Goddamn.*" He refused to say anything more about it.

Margaret decided to write to some of the young men in the neighborhood who'd been drafted or had volunteered to serve. The mother of Norman Capanna, who was one of her neighbors, provided his military address, along with stationery and stamps. Margaret wrote to him as often as she could. Lena thought it was a waste of time, but didn't dare tell the little girl not to write to him. Lena's patriotism was dubious, but she didn't want the entire neighborhood to know. She even refused to write to her family in Italy; she had Margaret handle that chore, too. Lena sent care packages filled with clothes or envelopes stuffed with money to them. Margaret had to lug the boxes to town and to give Lena a correct accounting of what it had cost to send them.

The little girl tried to make sense of Lena's attitude and why she treated her so poorly, but there didn't seem to be any answers. Worse still, she wondered why Uncle Charlie tolerated it.

9. Margaret and Norman

Charlie and Lena's relationship puzzled Margaret. They argued a lot and often directed their vitriol at her. They wouldn't speak for days, their long faces creating a never-ending tension in the house. It was a new experience for her. Although her parents may have had disagreements, she had never heard or witnessed anything resembling an argument between them; they certainly never yelled at her. Margaret's home life had been calm, quiet, and nurturing. Not anymore. The constant threats made her feel as though she was always off-balance.

Margaret had tenuous, complicated relationships with Lena's extended family. Lucia, Lena's niece, let it slip that Lena had given her Margaret's Shirley Temple glass. Margaret wondered what had happened to it. Rosa had purchased a box of Bisquick just to get the included promotional glass because she knew how much her little girl loved Shirley Temple's movies. Papa had brought it to her when she was sick at Elena's house. The glass had been packed among her things when she came to California after the Orphan's Court hearing. She had found it wrapped neatly in newspapers, so that it wouldn't break, but it had gone missing from her dresser drawer.

Lucia could have easily told Margaret that she had the glass and would keep it for her. But the girl, who was an only daughter, was spoiled and selfish. Margaret knew she had to tread lightly with her because Lucia would tell Aunt Lena about her plans or any perceived indiscretions.

Since Lucia tended to be a gossip and know-it-all, Margaret simply would listen and let her talk. One day, she told Margaret that Uncle Charlie and Aunt Lena had an arranged marriage. Lena and Lucia's father, Fausto, were siblings. Many years earlier, Fausto convinced Lena to come to America. Charlie, who was single, worked in the mine with Fausto. Fausto told Charlie about his unmarried sister, and Charlie agreed to marry her. While some of those kinds of unions work out, this one didn't. They hated each other. They shared common traits, like believing they were superior to everyone, degrading people behind their backs, and being rude. Charlie's friends teased him incessantly about marrying an old woman. Lena continually remarked how Italy was better than America, a dig at Charlie's proud WWI service. Fausto's wife, Almerinda, liked to say that Charlie was gasoline and Lena liked to light the match. Margaret knew that it was true. She grew to understand that it was a loveless marriage of convenience: Charlie had a woman to take care of him, and Lena had a man to support her. There wasn't any affection or goodwill between them, and the little girl felt the impact of their disappointment and loathing.

Margaret bore it as best she could. School was her refuge, and her teachers took note of her intelligence. She was an honor student at East Pike Run High School, which was right around the corner from their house on High Street. Margaret worked hard and finished third in her class. She tried to have a normal high school experience, ignoring Lena and Charlie as much as possible. She made it through high school with only two dresses to her name, which caused her to feel self-conscious and unhappy about her appearance. Students and teachers were kind to her, and she knew they had an inkling of what was happening at home. She wondered what her childhood friends were like now, and she realized they were getting ready to graduate from Cathedral High School. Margaret longed to see them and often imagined what her life would have been like if Mama hadn't died.

Lena and Charlie's arranged marriage took place in June 1921.

When she was a senior, her classmates were abuzz. It was time to order class rings. Margaret didn't dare to get her hopes up, but then she decided to ask Uncle Charlie if she could have ten dollars to purchase a ring. She'd learned to ask him questions over supper, when he was busy eating. She regretted the words as soon as she uttered them.

"Ten dollars?" Charlie said. "Do you think we're made of money? You don't need a ring."

And with that, Margaret knew she wouldn't receive one. When the day came for her classmates to be fitted for theirs, she watched from her desk, fighting back tears. Margaret was the only member of the East Pike Run Class of 1945 to not receive a ring. She kept telling herself that it was a small thing, but her life seemed to be filled with disappointments over small things.

Several teachers and members of the community knew about her situation and tried to help, but they were thwarted at every attempt. Margaret had confided in one of her teachers, Miss Johnson, about Rosa's dream for her to be a teacher. It had become Margaret's dream, too. California was the home of California State College, one of the finest teacher prep colleges in the state. Miss Johnson spoke with some officials at the college, and they arranged a full scholarship for her. A professor was impressed with Margaret's high school transcript. She offered tutoring services in return for Margaret doing light housework for her. Margaret was thrilled but apprehensive. What could go wrong? It wasn't as though she were going to ask Charlie and Lena to pay her tuition. She wouldn't even have to live on campus – it was only a block away. She could still do all the chores Lena had for her.

Miss Johnson walked Margaret home one day after school. Charlie had worked midnight shift, and he was sitting on the front porch.

Margaret graduated from East Pike Run High School in 1945.
Neither her uncle nor her aunt attended the ceremony.

Norman Capanna in a formal military portrait.
He served in the Army Air Corps in England during WWII.

"Hi, Mr. Angelo. I'd like to speak with you and Mrs. Angelo for a minute."

"Did she do something wrong?"

"No, sir. As a matter of fact, she's been doing everything right."

Charlie, wearing his usual scowl, called for Lena. She stepped onto the porch.

"What now?"

"I wanted to let you and Mr. Angelo know that Margaret has received a full scholarship to California State College. She can be a teacher, just like her mother hoped. It's become her dream, too. It won't cost you—"

"Only whores go to college," Lena said. "She doesn't need college. Get off our porch." She stared at Margaret. "And you, get in the house!"

Charlie never said a word but smirked his approval. Margaret was unable to speak. She went inside and wept yet again. It all seemed hopeless. Margaret had no idea what she was going to do now or if she would ever be able to leave. She felt trapped.

Margaret graduated from East Pike Run High School. She attended the ceremony alone, watching while her classmates' families congratulated them. Charlie and Lena, who never celebrated any holidays or birthdays, certainly weren't going to acknowledge this milestone in the young girl's life.

She received some money as graduation gifts and, defying Lena, used it to get out of the house. Margaret couldn't go far, but she took the train to Charleroi or Brownsville and went window shopping. On one trip to Charleroi, she ventured into the G.C. Murphy, and it reminded her of the store in Oakland that she and Rosa had frequently visited. There was a Murphy's in California, but this one was larger and had one significant difference – it included a lunch counter. Margaret looked at the menu, overwhelmed by the selections. Then, she saw something on the menu that sounded exotic – a tuna fish sandwich. She'd never eaten tuna before, so she ordered it. She was intrigued by the taste and enjoyed it so much that she vowed to have it again as soon as possible.

Margaret in undated photos in the front yard and backyard on High Street.

Even though Margaret was eighteen now, Charlie and Lena kept a tight rein on her. They controlled almost every aspect of her life. She'd take babysitting jobs or small housecleaning jobs for pocket money, but she didn't envision much of a future for herself.

One chilly fall morning when Margaret was working on a crochet project, Lena told her that she would have to paint the kitchen, bedrooms, and all the stairways. Margaret had never held a paintbrush, let alone painted an entire room. Even though they were thrifty, Charlie usually hired professional painters every few years to keep the house looking nice. Lena insisted on enamel paint, which was thick and dried fast. It took weeks, but Margaret finally completed the chore.

Much to her chagrin, Lena then insisted that she stain all the stairs and woodwork throughout the house. Margaret readily complied.

To pass time and to avoid her aunt and uncle, she engaged in solitary activities in her bedroom. Remembering Rosa's intricate and beautiful crocheted pieces, Margaret taught herself how to crochet. She also read all that she could: *Hamlet*, everything by the Bronte sisters, *Little Women*, Mark Twain, *Nancy Drew*, and *The Hardy Boys*, to name a few.

As Margaret approached twenty-one, she did have something to look forward to: she'd receive her parents' estate. Over the years, she'd dreamed of using it to attend school. Instead, it would finance her escape to a better life.

Unbeknownst to her, and before she could arrange to see an accounting of the estate, Uncle Charlie stepped in. He and a local lawyer filled out the paperwork and signed her signature, and all she saw was a check…for almost nothing. All her father's hard work, all her mother's sacrifices, were gone.

Margaret was furious. It was the one time that Uncle Charlie didn't smirk or walk away.

"Neither of you had any right to do that!" she said. "Those papers were in my name. I was supposed to sign them. I wanted to see the accounting. Where did it all go? There's nothing left! Where are the papers?"

Charlie bore the brunt of her fury, but like always, he refused to answer. She knew the account had to have been drained in less than eight years, but she didn't know how. She hadn't received any new clothes or decent food since she was a child, when her mother had cared for her.

Margaret struggled mightily with the disappointment, but she learned an important lesson: she had to speak up for herself. She had been worried about losing family, but that wasn't a concern any longer.

In some strange way she loved them, even while resenting them. She couldn't make sense of it, but she pushed it to the back of her mind.

Margaret began looking for a job. Whenever she received an offer, Lena called her a whore. Finally, at the age of twenty-seven, Margaret heard about a good paying job close to home. She worked up the courage to apply, and she was soon working as an operator at Bell Telephone in Brownsville, PA. Margaret took the bus, worked all day, then rode it home in the evening. She knew everyone on her route down Pennsylvania Avenue to the house on High Street, and they all greeted her as she walked home. She dawdled and talked as much as she wanted. Lena never said a word to Margaret about any of it. She knew better. After Margaret's confrontation with Charlie, Lena realized she was losing control of her. Margaret sensed her growing independence, too, and exerted it.

Margaret made many friends at work, and it was an exciting time for her. One of her new friends, Luella, talked about going to New York. Margaret had never considered it, but she was caught up in Luella's excitement. A former neighbor of Luella's, Betsy, had recently moved there, and invited them, along with Luella's sister, Bernice, to visit. They made the trip, overdressed country girls who stuck out like sore thumbs in the bustling metropolis. They dined at the Rainbow Room and saw a taping of the Ed Sullivan Show, featuring operatic singer and actress, Lily Pons. Betsy had connections. She gave a sealed envelope to Luella and told her to ask for Harry at the backdoor of the studio. Luella did as she was told, and soon she, Margaret, and Bernice were ushered in. They were seated in the front row of the balcony. After the broadcast, a page asked them to follow him. They returned to the backdoor, where Harry was waiting. He told them to stay put and disappeared back inside. Soon, out came Ed Sullivan himself, who greeted the girls and conversed for a few minutes. It turned out Harry was Ed's manager, and Betsy knew him.

Margaret was having a great time and genuinely enjoying herself. She was tasting freedom and independence on her own terms for the first time. She was relieved to be away from her aunt and uncle, whose unkindness seemed to know no bounds.

She returned to California, determined to see more of the world. When the call went out at the Brownsville Bell office for experienced operators who would be trained to work the overseas switchboard in Philadelphia, Margaret leapt at the chance. One of her co-workers, Elaine, wanted to go too, so they planned the move together.

In the days before Margaret was to leave California, Charlie and Lena expressed their displeasure by pouting and not speaking to her. Margaret packed her few belongings in a newly purchased suitcase. She walked out the front door with a loud, "Goodbye!" Neither her aunt nor uncle responded.

Fortunately, Bell was protective of the young women who worked for them. They made sure Margaret and Elaine were in an apartment in the Center City neighborhood that was not only close to work but safe.

Margaret thrived as an overseas operator, handling calls for the likes of John Kelly, Grace Kelly's father. She saved her money and was able to purchase some nice clothes and prepare nutritious meals for herself. She was even able to fly home to visit sporadically. She became ill on one flight because of some bad turbulence, but a kind gentleman helped her to the airport bar and bought her a ginger ale. He was an older businessman, who was catching a connecting flight to Chicago. He gave Margaret his card. Once he was sure she was all right, he ran to catch his next flight. Margaret laughed to herself, thinking if Lena knew she would call her names for letting a man buy her a ginger ale.

California seemed so much smaller now. She loved Sis and her other friends, but it was a different world. Still, she had good reason to return: She and Norman, the soldier she had written to during WWII, had fallen in love; all the correspondence had an unexpected effect. Norman was wise to Lena's true nature. Margaret confided in him about her situation, and he had told her long ago that she needed to stand up for herself, years before she had the confidence to do it. He finished his tour of duty in WWII (chiefly in England) and returned home to work on the railroad and then in the coal mines with his father. He visited her in Philadelphia and asked her to give up her burgeoning career to get married. She didn't want to move back and implored him to move to Philadelphia instead, but he was concerned about finding a job. Love won out. She moved back to California, and they were married on October 3, 1957.

Margaret and Norman's wedding portrait, October 3, 1957.

Norman worked in the coal mines and on the open hearth at the Clairton Works, the great steel mill along the Monongahela River. In 1960, their daughter was born. They named me Rosemary, after Rosa. In 1962, their son Peter Joseph was born. Pete was named after his grandfathers.

Margaret hadn't had any contact with Papa since Uncle Charlie chased him away. When I was born, she made some phone calls and discovered that he was staying with some extended family on South Bouquet. He was preparing to return to Italy. Margaret and Norman made their way to Oakland. Papa got to meet and hold his step granddaughter before he left. Margaret struggled with the words, and Papa was nervous, but she told him goodbye and asked him to write to her from Italy. It was the last time they saw each other.

In January 1962, just a few short months before Pete was born, Lena died. Margaret experienced a mix of emotions, but she felt mostly relief. After she'd confronted her Uncle Charlie about her parents' estate, he had stopped being quite as gruff to her, although he still had little to say. Margaret had taken to calling him Dad, more as a show of respect for who he was than the place he held in her life. She understood better what he had gone through with his wife, although she realized that it didn't excuse his treatment of her. Lena, however, treated her no differently. She was arrogant and demanding and even asked Margaret to name me Michelina, after her. Mom declined.

Norman and Margaret set up house in McKeesport, near the Clairton Works. Soon he was laid off, and they moved to Coal Center, PA, just outside California, where the cost of living was cheaper and where family was nearby to help with the children. When the mill fired up again, he commuted to his job.

After Lena died, Uncle Charlie asked Norman and Margaret to move in. Margaret was against the idea. She abhorred the thought of returning to the house that held so many awful memories for her. But Norman insisted, seeing it as an opportunity to have more space for their growing family. Margaret relented, but soon it was apparent that

Norman and Charlie didn't get along. It was one thing to visit his uncle by marriage; it was another to live with him. They didn't speak, and Charlie watched baseball on his new color television with the volume turned as high as he could to annoy Norman.

On the upside, Margaret now had free reign of the house. Lena had never done any decorating, so Margaret did the best she could. She cooked and baked to her heart's content and focused on her children. She thrived without anyone telling her what to do. Although there was tension between her husband and uncle, she was used to the strain between Charlie and Lena. She didn't like it, but she knew how to cope.

Her dearest friend, Sis, married and moved away; the rest of Sis' family eventually moved away, too. Pauline and her husband, John, purchased their home. When I was five, Pauline asked Margaret if she'd like for me to attend church. Margaret was a lapsed Catholic. She'd attended the Catholic Church in Coal Center when she first moved to California, but she hadn't given it much thought in a long time. The Christian Church (Disciples of Christ) was right over the hill in Phillipsburg, the little immigrant mining community tucked between the Monongahela River and the edge of the college campus. Pauline's son, who was the same age as me, went every Sunday. Soon, I was attending, too.

Margaret, who'd never forgotten Rosa's love for her, followed her example. She was a caring, involved mother. Her children's interest in church sparked her interest, too. In 1967, Margaret made a commitment to Jesus Christ. She worked hard for the church and community, and she did her best to live up to the beliefs she embraced.

Uncle Charlie sporadically doted on his brother's grandchildren. He read to me from the newspaper and taught me how to read from it while I sat on his lap. Before I'd entered kindergarten, I'd learned enough to read the newspaper to him. He bought us bicycles, and he surprised me with a guitar for my sixth birthday. Uncle Charlie taught Pete about gardening and how to properly trim his immaculate hedge fence and arched gate that bordered the property.

Rosemary and Pete Capanna in 1967.

It appeared that Charlie wanted to purge memories, any trace of his past, or perhaps any evidence of wrongdoing. As he grew older, he burned documents, letters, and photos for no apparent reason.

One day, Margaret heard Pauline yelling for her, and she ran outside onto the porch to find Uncle Charlie slumped over near his hanging planter, which he'd been cleaning. She could tell by his face that he'd had a stroke. He tried to tell her something, and she told him it was OK. He died the next day, November 10, 1972, at the age of 81.

Most of the connections to Margaret's past were gone or she hadn't spoken with them in years, or she'd simply lost track; she just didn't know much about them. Uncle Nick and Uncle Mike, Giuseppe's brothers, died within a month of each other in 1960. She vaguely knew Uncle Nick's children. Throughout the years, she had visited her distant cousins, Laura and Flora, in Canonsburg with Uncle Charlie, but he refused to see Nick while he was there. Margaret was conditioned by years of this behavior and learned not to visit, either. She didn't know why; she just did as she had been taught, and she continued to do so for most of her life. Uncle Charlie had treated Mike as shabbily as he had Nick, although she did get to know at least three of Mike's children quite well: Pearl, Doris, and Clarence, who was known as "Slim." They lived closer to California than Uncle Nick's family did, so it was easier to interact with them. Margaret and Pearl grew close when Pearl moved to Pennsylvania Avenue. Slim was the most gregarious of the bunch and made a point of visiting Margaret and Norman often at the High Street house.

Overall, life was good. Margaret had the family that she wanted, even though she was unsure of her own heritage. When she asked Uncle Charlie about her parents, he wouldn't answer, so she learned to stop asking. She meekly questioned her distant cousins about her parents, but they weren't interested in explaining her ancestry. Margaret didn't push for answers.

To complicate matters, Lena had taken pleasure in lying to Margaret about her family. As Margaret grew older, she had ceased hiding her correspondences with her cousin, Victor, but she once again lost track of him. Lena had told her that it didn't matter because they weren't cousins anyway. Margaret had also written a few letters to a gentleman in Quadri, whom she believed to be an uncle, her mother's brother. She'd gotten his address from someone, but she wasn't sure whom. Lena had said he was really a cousin; that Rosa had just thought of him like a brother.

Lena sowed doubt, and Margaret reaped uncertainty.

Although details were scant, there were a few. She knew her parents were from Quadri; this was indisputable. Mama and Papa had often pointed out who they knew from their commune in the *Old Country*. She knew that her paternal grandmother's first name was Fedele because Uncle Charlie had a large framed photo of her hanging in the house and had mentioned it to her. Margaret had also seen her own birth certificate – her parents had originally named her Fedele, but it was changed to Margherita. She had no idea why. How could she? She didn't even know her mother's maiden name. She'd learned to live with the notion that she might never have any answers to the endless questions that haunted her.

10. Discoveries

I'd like to share with you how I uncovered the information you've read thus far and how I compiled this book. The journey of discovery produced answers that have changed several lives.

In my late teens, I began asking Mom about her early life. I knew she was an orphan; it was a fuzzy thing to me, given that she was my mother. It didn't seem unusual or strange.

Thirty-five years ago, we tried to learn more about her family. It seemed an impossible task. California State College (now California University of Pennsylvania) had some of the Pittsburgh newspapers on microfilm, so we spent hours searching through old papers, looking for death notices and obituaries. Even though we knew the date of her father's death and the year of her mother's, it was an intimidating task, and we were unsuccessful. We drove to Panther Hollow and South Oakland. I saw the house on Pier Street, where Rosa had died. We ventured down into the Hollow, onto Boundary Street. All the houses from her childhood were still standing, and still are. I imagined Rosa, Giuseppe, Papa, and Margherita, working and playing and living there. I was overcome with emotion, a strong sense of family, and by our history.

The University of Pittsburgh was overrunning most of Oakland. As families moved out and headed to the suburbs, the houses were converted to student housing. I wanted to knock on doors, but Margaret was reluctant, so we left. As overwhelmed as I was, it was indescribably difficult for her.

One day, in frustration, I went to the public library and looked through the Pittsburgh phone directory. I found Elena's number, jotted it down, and went home and called her. She wasn't pleased at all. In the forty years since the courtroom drama, her husband's family-run business had provided them with a comfortable living, and they'd become a prominent family in Pittsburgh. It meant nothing to me; I knew what she was. I told her that I simply wanted to know about my grandparents, what kind of people they were, things like that. There was a long pause, and then she quietly said that they were good people who loved to garden and who kept to themselves. I thanked her, and she asked for my mom. I handed the phone to her, and I knew immediately that I'd made a mistake. I was sitting across the table from my mom, and I could hear Elena's voice rising through the phone. She wasn't happy that I had called, and she wondered if mom had put me up to it.

"I didn't raise my children that way. She's curious about her grandparents."

"You forget how much I helped you and took care of you."

"I'm still waiting on that cup of tea."

And with that, Mom hung up. We didn't speak of Elena again for many years.

Shortly after that, I wrote to Vital Records for a copy of Giuseppe's death certificate. Rosa had told Mom his birth and death dates, so it wasn't difficult to request. From it, I learned that Uncle Charlie had been there when his brother had died – he'd signed the certificate as a witness to his death. His father's name was Domenico, and his mother's name was, indeed, Fedele. Her maiden name read "Diplata," which was intriguing. But we didn't have anything else to go on, and I didn't know how to trace Mom's ancestry. The genealogical books that I borrowed from the library were more scholarly than helpful. They were also geared more toward American heritage. We were of Italian descent, and we needed information that was relatively new for the United States, less than one hundred years old. The only other option I could think of was to hire a genealogist, but that was too expensive.

Seeing that we were hitting walls, we accepted that we might never know much.

The 1980s and 1990s rolled by. Time was passing quickly, and the few family members Mom knew died. First Pearl, then Slim. Her distant cousins in Canonsburg, Flora and Laura, passed, then Laura's husband, John, died. So did her childhood best friend, Sis.

A coal miner and lifelong smoker, Norman developed black lung, a mining disease caused by inhaling coal dust. He was also diagnosed with red lung, from breathing in the searing heat while working on the open hearth at the Clairton Works. Emphysema complicated those conditions, and Norman passed in 2002.

In 2004, I saw Ancestry.com's television commercials and decided to try it for a few months. It wasn't expensive at all, especially compared to hiring a genealogist. I didn't have much luck digging up information, though. I decided to let it go, consoled Mom, and wondered why she couldn't be blessed with at least a few answers to the many questions she'd had for most of her life. It only seemed fair given the pain and abuse she had suffered after Rosa died.

Another ten years passed, and in 2014, Ancestry aired some intriguing television commercials. At first, I was resistant, but I told Mom I'd try one more time. I signed up again, and she hovered over me while I typed in her father's name. We had several hits, but I knew immediately that Ancestry had added more records: her father's death certificate came up in the searches. It was an exciting moment; little did we know we were in for many more.

I clicked the link to information for the Pennsylvania Death Certificate database and discovered it was available for the years up to 1964. Rosa had to be in there, too. I searched under her second married name, and the certificate came up. This is how we learned that Rosa died exactly one week after Margaret's twelfth birthday – Mom didn't have any recollection of that, most likely due to the trauma. Rosa's father was listed as "Gaetano Daluisis" and her mother as unknown.

We went back to the main search, and I entered "Rosa Daluisis," with Pittsburgh as a place she lived and Quadri as her place of birth. There were quite a few results with many variations on the last name. We knew she'd passed in 1939, so I eliminated everyone who was still alive after that date or who had died prior to it.

We were getting close.

I clicked on an Ellis Island record for a "Rosa D'Aluisio." The age matched, but her destination address in Pittsburgh did not. Still, something told me I was on the right track, so I flagged the record and moved onto the next link. It was a passport application. As I read it, the hair on the back of my neck stood on end – I was certain it was my grandmother's passport application. She was coming to Pittsburgh to be with her husband. She was coming to be with Giuseppe.

Mom and I read the application and wept. Her memories and the stories she was told were being confirmed, piece by piece. We recognized that small miracles were taking place.

I noticed a handwritten number on Rosa's Ellis Island record matched a typewritten number on her immigration record. This was, indeed, the same person.

Mom was thrilled, and so was I. I continued to build the family tree, sorting out the various cousins. Four of the six D'Arcangelo brothers had come to America. Only Uncle Charlie hadn't had any children. In my mind, I thought that Flora and Laura's father was one of the six brothers, especially since they resided in Canonsburg. He wasn't. I turned my attention to Uncle Nick, who made my mom feel special and loved at a time when she so desperately needed it. All his children had passed away, except for one: Ada. I felt badly about it; over the years it never occurred to me that I could have asked Uncle Nick's children if they had any insight about my mom and her situation. I asked Mom why she hadn't been in touch with her cousins.

"Uncle told me not to."

"Why?"

She thought about it for a while before responding, "I don't know."

The fact is, Mom did what she was told. Uncle Charlie drilled into her to steer clear of his brothers, so she did. She obeyed him because she wanted to protect the only family she thought she had, as terrible as Charlie and Lena were. I realized that she also might be suffering from Post-Traumatic Stress Disorder; she certainly matched the criteria.[3] It was sad and disturbing, and it had robbed her of the joy of knowing her uncles, aunts, and cousins.

Ada was still alive, though, and that could be a chance for Margaret to at least get to know her. I easily found her number online. I implored Mom to call.

"I don't know if she'll want to talk to me."

"You won't know if you don't call."

Deep down, and rightfully so, Mom was terrified of the possible rejection. She wasn't even sure Ada would remember her. It took a few months for her to work up the courage and make the call.

"Is this Ada DeAngelo?"

"Yes," Ada said, drawing out the word as if questioning why someone was asking for her by her maiden name.

"You're Nick DeAngelo's daughter?"

"Yes."

"This is your cousin Margaret, from California."

The phone went silent. I saw a flash of concern cross Mom's face.

"Oh, my God. I was just telling my niece that I wondered whatever happened to you!"

Ada DeAngelo Pifferetti and Margaret met for the first time
in more than sixty years on May 28, 2014.

Ada was overjoyed, and Mom was now in touch with her last remaining paternal first cousin. Ada was the one who recounted about the day they had visited Uncle Charlie's house, all those years ago. Mom had no memory of it. Ada told Mom that the last time they saw each other was more than sixty years earlier, about a year after Ada's mom had died in 1953. Mom did remember that. Uncle Charlie had someone drive him, Lena, and Mom to Canonsburg to visit with Flora and Laura. For some reason, on a whim, he directed the driver right to Nick's house. Lena was furious. Mom remembered that visit well, particularly the joy Uncle Nick and Ada had when they saw her. Margaret also met Grace, another cousin, for the first time. They got along famously. Mom's recollection of this event came easily, most likely because the visit took place after she had started working at Bell Telephone and had asserted her independence from Charlie and Lena.

In many ways, in Ada, Margaret found the sibling she never had. Ada, at 84, was just three years younger. She was kind, warm, funny, and always happy to chat with her long-lost cousin. Ada missed her sisters, and Margaret filled that emptiness a bit. It was a wonderful relationship, a heartwarming gift for two lonely, elderly women.

Ada told us what she knew about the D'Arcangelo family and a story or two about my grandfather. Although he'd passed before she was born, she'd heard tales from her father and sisters. She also bore witness to Charlie's odd behavior. Ada and I talked for hours. One evening, she told me she'd wondered why Mom had never been in touch. I explained to her the abuse that Mom endured and how Uncle Charlie had instilled in her the idea that she should never, ever visit Nick or Mike or their families. Ada cried over this bit of information. After that, she told us that her father wanted Mom to live with them, but it was arranged that she would live with Charlie and Lena instead because they didn't have any children. Ada always made sure to emphasize to my mom that Uncle Nick, Aunt Carmela, and their family *wanted* her. Surely, Mom would have had a better life if she'd been sent to live with either Uncle Nick or Uncle Mike. Of his three siblings, Charlie was the one who visited with Giuseppe the most. He also visited Antonio and Rosa after Giuseppe died (he loved attending those baseball games at Forbes Field). Because of this, he was the uncle who was considered closest to Margaret. He may have been the most familiar uncle, but he most certainly was not the best suited to the task of raising a child.

Mom and I went to Orphan's Court at the Allegheny County Courthouse to try and learn more about the events that transpired in her childhood. I'd discovered the docket numbers for both of my grandparents' wills, and I knew there had to be supporting documents included. The clerk gathered our reference numbers and returned with two stacks of papers. One stack was for Giuseppe, the other for Rosa. It was like touching the Dead Sea Scrolls…the papers weren't brittle, but I realized that we were the first people to examine them since 1939-40. The passage of time and the pain of my mother's childhood was never lost on me.

Giuseppe died intestate, and I found some information about it. There wasn't much, but it gave an accounting of his large estate and how Mom was his sole heir. We also confirmed Rosa's desire to hold it in trust for Margaret. Rosa's will was in Italian, with the translation provided by Elena's sister. We also found Mom's baptismal certificate, which indicated that she'd been baptized at Immaculate Conception and not St. Paul, like she'd always thought.

We didn't have enough time to copy the papers, so I took a few photos of them. Not knowing where to park, I had to settle for the lot across the street, which cost about thirty dollars for a half hour. I didn't have much time, so I ran upstairs to the clerk's office to see if I could find Antonio and Rosa's ledger entry for their marriage license. I'd learned from the 1930 census that they were married, so I knew it had to have occurred after February 1929 (when Giuseppe died) and before April 1930, when the census was dated. I found them listed as Antonio D'Amico and Rosa D'Amico. They'd gotten Rosa's last name wrong. Now I had the information needed to order the marriage license online.

I inspected the marriage license closely when it arrived, and it seemed that Antonio and Rosa may not have understood what names they were being asked to provide. No worries, because now I had new information.

I made a habit of regularly searching on my grandfather's name at Ancestry, using variations of the spelling. One day, a death certificate from 1925 came up for their stillborn child. The baby didn't have a name; he was simply called "Baby D'Angelo." It was depressing to see the cause of death, knowing what my grandmother had written to Lena about it. I continued examining the certificate. The child was buried in St. Peter's Cemetery on Lemington Avenue. We wanted to know if there was a burial plot that we could visit, so I called the cemetery to see if they had any record of it. I left a few messages on their machine, but no one returned my calls. My cousin is a funeral director. I asked him to call the cemetery and leave a vague message, thinking that he might be able to get their attention and receive a return call. No luck.

In my frustration, I discussed what was happening with my friend, James Corrie. Jim told me that he was familiar with the cemetery. He drove us there one sunny morning, and we looked around for a marker for my mom's brother. We couldn't find any, and the cemetery's caretaker had pinned a "Do not disturb" notice on his door.

I did more investigating and found that the cemetery, and the church on its grounds, were under the auspices of the Church of Christ. I contacted them on Facebook, and they gave me the phone number of the church's pastor. I reached him, and we had a lovely discussion. The church was barely functioning, and the building served more as a chapel for funerals. Fortunately, he gave me the email address of someone who knew about the cemetery records. I wrote her, and she was helpful – at first. She told me that stillborn and premature babies were often buried at the ends of rows or in odd places where an adult couldn't fit, and those graves were usually unmarked. Since I knew when he died, she told me, she might be able to calculate where he was buried. She'd been working on this sort of thing for a while. It was encouraging news. She even sent me a printout of interments that included the name Baby D'Angelo.

After several months, I wrote back and asked if she'd had time to sort out where he might be buried. I told her that my family had discussed it, and we'd consider placing a small marker on the gravesite (or at least near it) and another on behalf of all the children in unmarked graves there. Those last comments must not have sat too well with her because she told me she had no idea where he was buried. I wrote back and apologized if we'd overstepped, and she never responded again. It was disappointing, but there wasn't anything I could do about it. At least we know that he's there, and perhaps we'll place a marker someday, even if it's not on his actual gravesite.

11. Answers

I continued to flesh out the tree at Ancestry as best I could, happy that it resulted in a lovely, meaningful reunion with Ada. I felt as though I was beginning to run out of resources, but through Googling "Quadri" and looking for a list of residents, I guessed that my grandmother's last name was properly spelled "D'Aloisio." I knew from her death certificate that her father's name was Gaetano. I didn't know where to look next. It occurred to me to Google "Gaetano D'Aloisio, Quadri." I thought that perhaps I'd pull up some old records in Italy, given the Internet's global nature. However, the first link was to a Facebook profile. I sent a friend request and then used Google Translate to send a message.

"Ciao. I live in the United States. My grandparents were from Quadri. My maternal great grandfather's name was Gaetano D'Aloisio. Perhaps we're related."

He accepted my friend request and I received a warm message back, in Italian.

"I don't know if we're related or not, but I do know that I am Gaetano D'Aloisio, and I do know that I am from Quadri!"

I appreciated his sense of humor. His earnest response made me curious about Quadri, so I Googled the town. I discovered that with Google Maps Street View I could "walk" the streets and explore. I marveled at the notion that I was digitally negotiating the very places that generations of my mom's family had walked.

Another Google search brought up some YouTube videos. I was curious, so I began watching them. They were fun – there were feste (church festivals to honor saints) and scenes from the town's truffle festival. They were in Italian, so I didn't understand them, but Mom did some translating. One of the videos was beautifully shot and edited; it looked as though it had been produced by a professional. I left a message in Italian in the video's comment section, explaining how much I'd enjoyed it and that my maternal grandparents were from Quadri. A short time later, I received a response to my comment.

"Can you tell me more? I would like to see if I can sort out your connection."

I'd already put together a website with the family tree at quadrichieiti.com, so I sent him the link. It included Rosa, Giuseppe, and Antonio, but only one generation beyond them: Giuseppe's mother and father, and Rosa's father and unknown mother. I thought that, with some luck, someone might be searching for the same information that I was trying to find and pull up the website.

I could tell by his avatar that the person I was corresponding with was an older gentleman. I directed him to the website. A few days later, he replied again.

"After doing a long search in the genealogy, I've discovered that we're second cousins!"

Raffaele, the videographer, was the grandson of Ermete, one of the six D'Arcangelo brothers who'd remained in Italy. He lived in Paris, but spent half the year in Quadri. I happened to catch him while he was there. We exchanged emails. He described for me how he was overcome with emotion to find such close cousins in America. I assured Raffaele that we were overcome, too.

Raffaele had indeed researched the genealogy. He sent me a family tree that he compiled directly from the comune records. It wasn't complete, but it went straight back several generations and filled in some details that we may have never discovered otherwise – and we now knew the true names and birthdates of the six D'Arcangelo brothers. Rosa's mother's name was Domenica D'Amico. Giuseppe's mother's name was Fedele Di Pilato.

Not only had Raffaele traced some of our roots, he also put us in touch with a second cousin on Rosa's side: Vincenzo D'Aloisio. Margaret had corresponded with Vincenzo's grandfather (also named Vincenzo) all those years ago. He was the one Lena claimed wasn't truly Rosa's brother, and that Rosa had simply thought of him "as" a brother. When Mom heard the news, she told me that, most of all, she was grateful that she'd referred to him as "Zio Vincenzo" (Uncle Vincenzo) when she wrote to him. She kept the letter that he wrote to her after I was born in 1960. Mom had sent him five dollars and my photo, and she explained that she named me after Rosa. It touched the old man, who lost his sister twice – first, when she left for America and then when she died. In his letter, he related that Mom's stepfather, Antonio, had made it back to Quadri and sent his greetings. Mom wrote to Vincenzo a few more times, but he never responded. Through his grandson, we learned that he had fallen ill shortly after his last letter to Mom and died a few years later. I sent a photo of the letter, and the grandson printed out a copy, which he framed and keeps near his favorite chair in his living room.

And the Gaetano D'Aloisio I'd friended on Facebook? His father was also a grandson of Rosa's brother, making him a great grandson, and Margaret's third cousin.

Suddenly, Mom was up to her ears in cousins! She never had many family members, and now she was drowning in them. It was funny, touching, and wonderful. They loved us, and they let us know it. We were emailing and messaging with them. Vincenzo, who was in his mid-seventies, wanted to Skype with us. His wife, Letizia Casasanta, joined us for the first of what have become regular video chat sessions.

Through our Quadri connections, we learned that we have family scattered not only across Italy but throughout the world: Canada, France, Germany, Australia, and South America, to name a few places. Many of the younger generation speak perfect English, and some have traveled extensively.

Uncle Vincenzo D'Aloisio and his wife, Luisa D'Amico in an undated photo.
Photo courtesy of Vincenzo D'Aloisio.

Uncle Vincenzo's letter to Margaret after Rosemary was born in 1960.

Our world was rapidly expanding. While we were grateful to learn Rosa's maiden name, confirm that Vincenzo was indeed my mom's uncle, and find our extended family, I couldn't shake a nagging feeling that I was missing something.

In the meantime, the friend who'd driven us to the cemetery, James Corrie, began working at the Allegheny County Courthouse. He'd become familiar with Mom's story and was hooked. Jim and his co-worker, Frank Morris, copied every document in the Orphan's Court records that pertained to Mom's case. Those records confirmed many things, including her tale of Elena wanting one-hundred dollars per month but only receiving ten dollars. Frank was hooked, too; he pursued a lead and researched and copied records from civil court proceedings that had taken place after my grandmother's death. Through those records, we learned that Mom's godparents, Sabatino and Giulia, had borrowed one thousand, one hundred dollars to purchase a house. Through other sources, we learned that Elena threatened them with legal action (there was a judgment in favor of Rosa's estate), got them to repay the loan, and pocketed it. The estate never received a dime.

Lawyers' fees ate away a bit of the estate over the eight years Mom waited to collect it, but not as much as one might expect.

Most importantly, the records revealed the horrific truth about why Margaret had been treated so poorly. Of course, she was to inherit the bulk of her parents' estate. According to Rosa's will, Antonio, who had lost so much, was to receive a slightly smaller inheritance and would collect the entire estate if anything happened to Margaret. But, he disclaimed it – technically, he declined to accept the money that Rosa left him. He wanted Margaret to have the full proceeds of her parents' estate. It was a thoughtful and kind act, confirmation not only of his love for Rosa and Margaret but for his cousin and best friend, Giuseppe, too. His gesture took him completely out of the inheritance line, leaving Margaret as the sole heir – and Elena knew it. With Antonio out of the picture, she saw her opportunity. If anything happened to Margaret, Elena, as executrix, could do whatever she liked with the estate. She (and her mother) starved and neglected the little girl, hoping that Margaret would die so that they could collect the proceeds. Antonio, who couldn't have recognized the legal consequences of his decision, only knew that Margaret was being mistreated. His intuitive distrust of Elena was well-founded.

What about Uncle Charlie and Aunt Lena? They had been receiving monies from the estate for Margaret's room and board; she never really benefitted from those payments, considering the lack of food and clothing. Many requests were made for additional monies for living expenses, and they were granted. In the end, Lena was generous to her family both in America and Italy, at the expense of my grandparents' estate – and my mom's general wellbeing and education.

Once again, I reviewed the documents I'd found on Ancestry. I was drawn to Rosa's passport application. I read it more carefully and realized several things. First, my grandfather had served in the U.S. military. That information was on the passport application. The application also stated that my grandmother was a U.S. citizen…but she had never visited the United States. I was able to answer those questions after some digging. So, what was bugging me now?

Suddenly, I realized what it was. I was able to "turn the page" on the digital document! I felt like a dummy. In my excitement, amid the flood of information I'd found, I hadn't turned the page to see what was on the back of it. Once I did, and to my great astonishment, staring back at me was my grandmother. I gaped in shocked disbelief. Yes, the quality of the photo was atrocious. It looked like a photocopy, and it was very small, but it was undeniably Rosa. My entire life, I'd seen the only photo Mom had of her parents hanging on the wall in the house on High Street. There was no doubt. I eagerly yelled for Mom. I took my laptop into the kitchen, and when she came in, I told her about the photo. I enlarged it on the screen as much as I could, and she burst into tears. Mom was gazing at the photo when something else dawned on me.

"Mom, what's today's date?"

"It's June twenty-eighth."

My grandmother's birthday was June twenty-eighth.

These sorts of "coincidences" became routine.

Encouraged, I thought I'd recheck the census to see if it offered any additional clues. I wasn't as rushed as I had been when I initially found it, so I thoroughly read every column. I saw there was a question in one column that I hadn't noticed before: "Personal description -- age of person at first marriage."

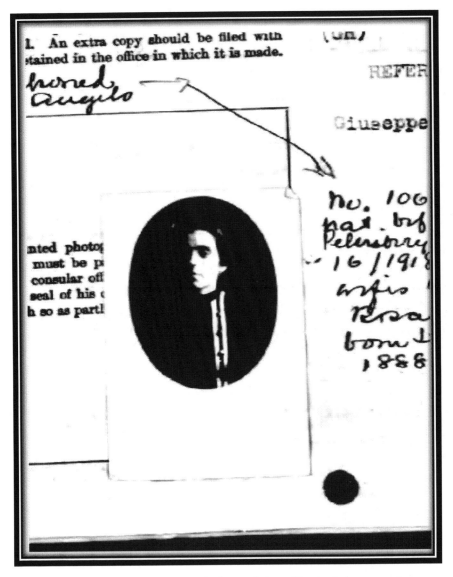

Rosa's passport photo, 1923. It is only the second photo of her that is known to exist.

Rosa and Giuseppe's estate accounting from the Allegheny County Courthouse, 1940. The total was bolstered by Rosa's life insurance policy ($500) and a judgment for the estate of $1100 against Margherita's godparents.

I knew how old Rosa was when she married Giuseppe, but Antonio's age wasn't adding up for his marriage to Rosa.

"Mom, was Antonio married before?"

"No. I don't think so. No."

Mom was certain he wasn't, then she was unsure, and I was altogether stumped. It was odd. Given his age, I thought that it was reasonable to believe that he must have been married to someone else before he married Rosa. I set it aside to give it more consideration.

I thought a lot about Antonio and decided to dig deeper. He had a very common Italian name; I'd found at least six people with the same name in the Pittsburgh area. I searched with variations, as I had with Giuseppe, and up came a death certificate. I held my breath as I read it, and realized that it was for Antonio's first wife, Rose. She died in 1926. I didn't understand the cause of death, so I asked some friends. Basically, her placenta had dropped after childbirth and she bled to death. It could happen immediately, within a few hours, or in a few weeks. Wait. She died after childbirth? Mom didn't know anything about Antonio having a child; she'd never known about a first wife, let alone a child.

I went to the death certificates database. I figured I'd go through them one-by-one and find the child's death certificate. I went through all of 1925 and 1926. When I didn't find anything, I went through 1927. Then 1928, and 1929. I tried 1924 and 1923. I was bewildered. The only thing I could think of was that the death certificate hadn't been filed for some reason, or perhaps it was misfiled or lost. There was no trace of the child, except on its mother's death certificate.

The certificate noted that Rose was buried in Calvary Cemetery, where Rosa and Giuseppe are. I drove over and stopped by the office. I asked if they could tell me where Rose was buried. One of the clerks went into a back room. Given the death date, she had to look in one of the old ledgers. She returned with a slip of paper with the plot number written on it.

"Oh, by the way," I said, "is a child also buried there?"

The clerk hesitated. "Um, yeah. There's someone buried with her."

That piece of information appeared to close the search. Rose's grave was in an old part of the cemetery, and it didn't have a marker. I knew the general area – it was on a hill above my grandfather's resting place. For the next year and a half, whenever we went to the cemetery, I made a point of going by Rose's plot and speaking a prayerful blessing:

"Hi, Rose. We know about you and your baby. You're not forgotten."

I thought about how tragic it was that Antonio had lost his first wife and child, then lost his second wife and child. He had to have been a shattered man.

We considered getting a small marker for Rose's grave, too. Antonio was a wonderful father to my mother; he literally saved her life. It would have been a small gesture of our love and esteem for him.

I began to write this book and wondered what sort of conclusion it would have. I thought it would end with Margaret and Ada reconnecting. That would have been a perfect, joyous ending, and we're grateful for the time we had with her. We love her dearly, and always will. But the story wasn't finished yet, not by a long shot.

We did Mom's DNA and discovered, sadly and much to our dismay, that Elena's mother and Giuseppe were third cousins. It added another layer of pain and sorrow to the scenario.

There were other matches, though, and we contacted some of them and received an occasional reply. One match we reached out to was Florence, Victor's sister. Victor and Margaret were indeed cousins – second cousins on Rosa's side, to be exact. I did some more detective work and discovered that Florence's grandmother, Carmella, and

Margaret's grandfather, Gaetano, were siblings. I was ecstatic to have solved this mystery for Mom. We made a call to Florence – I found her number online. She and Mom didn't know each other (Mom is seven years older), but she was excited to learn a little about the family on her father's side. Albert had passed away when she was a child in 1940, having been in ill health since he was wounded in WWI. He and Giuseppe boarded together on Boundary Street prior to being drafted. I happily sent her a photo of that building, along with other documents pertaining to her family's time in America.

I believed that I'd now completed the tale; I'd found everything Mom could ever know about her family in this lifetime.

In August of 2016, after 35 years of sporadic research and about three years of dedicated genealogical investigation, I needed to review the information I'd compiled on Ancestry to see how I could put it all together in a book. I opened my account and noticed a lot of "hint" leaves. I sighed; most of them weren't for our family. They were usually names whose spelling was close to ours. Something nudged me to look anyway, so I did. It was a hint for Rose, Antonio's first wife. I rolled my eyes; hints for her usually had to do with her sister. Rose died so young that there wasn't much information about her to be had. It was a family tree hint. I didn't expect to find anything I didn't already know, and sure enough, the tree listed Antonio, Rose, and…private. Private? What was a "private" listing doing under their names? I knew what it meant, but my eyes could hardly believe it. A "private" entry meant that the person was still alive. Could Antonio and Rose's child indeed have survived childbirth? If so, could that child still be alive in 2016?

I called for my mom and told her what I'd found. It was beyond surreal. I wrote to the person who managed the tree and told him that Antonio and Rose's child had a stepsister, and I wanted to contact the person whose entry was listed as "private" as soon as possible. I realized that, given the ages of the people involved, time was of the essence. I received a rude response and no information or offer to help, but I was determined, so I decided to sort it out for myself. The tree was public, so I clicked on the child's entry and did some digging. I discovered that the child was a woman. Her husband had died, so there was a public entry for him – and from that, I found her married surname. I did some Googling and pulled up what I believed to be her name and phone number.

She was in Munhall, PA, not far from us!

I was worried about calling; she was ninety-years-old. What if she wasn't in good health or was unaware of her history? What if she didn't know about her biological parents?

Additional searching revealed some names of individuals who I thought were her family. I found them on Facebook and sent private messages. The suspense was awful. It was a Friday. I told Mom that if they didn't respond I'd call the next day and take my chances.

The phone rang the evening of August 12, 2016. It was Patty, a woman I'd contacted on Facebook. She wasn't sure what my message was about or why I'd asked her to call – she hadn't thoroughly read it, she just knew that someone wrote to her, asking about her mother.

I asked if her grandfather's name was Antonio, and if her grandmother's name was Rose. Patty hesitatingly said yes. I explained that Antonio was my mother's stepfather, and that I believed our mothers were stepsisters, making us step cousins. It was a lot to absorb. There was a bit of stunned silence, and Patty asked me to repeat what I'd said, so that she could get it straight. Patty later revealed that her mother, Sara, claimed for years to have a sister, though she'd heard differently about our mothers' relationship. Sara was told that they were half-sisters. I explained that they weren't, and promised to provide some documentation. We chatted for a while and decided to keep in touch. We'd get together soon so that we could meet and talk more about our relationship.

Sisters: Sara and Margaret meet for the first time – September 4, 2016.

Patty also told us that while she was talking with me, Sara realized what the call was about and angrily yelled at Patty from her bedroom: "I told you I had a sister!" Sara, who'd been adopted by cousins, wasn't told about her adoption until she was in her fifties, when her adoptive mother was dying. It was thought best not to tell children that they were adopted. There was fear that the child might leave or that the biological parents might try to interfere or take the child back.

Over the years, Patty had made phone calls to residents in Oakland and Panther Hollow on Sara's behalf, trying to find someone who knew the true story of her birth or the whereabouts of her sister – or if a sister even existed. The inquiries were fruitless. A few months prior to our call, Patty had told Sara that she might have to accept that she wouldn't ever know the truth. They'd given up hope of ever finding any answers.

Sara was told some tall tales about her birth, which led her to believe that Antonio had abandoned her, returned to Italy, and had another daughter there. Parts of the story had some basis in fact, but Antonio hadn't abandoned Sara; he had no choice. Times were different then, and no one would have permitted a single man to raise a child on his own, especially an infant. It would have been impossible with his job in the mill, given the long hours he worked. Additionally, his wife's family may have blamed him for Rose's death, since she died in childbirth.

Sadly, Margaret and Sara experienced many of the same childhood abuses and traumas. The timing of their parents' deaths was gut-wrenching; if they'd occurred just a little differently, Margaret and Sara most likely would have grown up together, or at least known more about each other. It wouldn't have come close to compensating for what they'd lost, but at least they would've had each other.

Antonio D'Amico's grave portrait. Photo courtesy of Raffaele D'Amico.

Sara prayed faithfully that someday she and her sister would find each other, and they have. She and Margaret refer to themselves not as stepsisters but as sisters, and they are getting to know each other. While there is sadness in finding Sara this late in life, Margaret has been able to tell her about the kind of man her father truly was, and Sara has found peace in this. We love our new extended family and get together whenever we can.

Antonio returned to Italy in 1960, but only after a lifetime of work and heartbreak in America. It's impossible to imagine how he must have felt to be back in Quadri after everything that had occurred. He'd lost two wives and left behind a stepdaughter, as well as a biological daughter and grandchildren that he'd never know. He probably believed they'd never learn about him; that he'd lost everything he hoped to find in America. But they do know about him, and his descendants in the United States now number more than fifty – and counting. He has no immediate family left in Italy.

I asked Raffaele if anyone in the comune could tell us what happened to *la gaugliona's* beloved Papa, knowing that he had to have passed years ago. He responded with some photographs of Antonio's gravesite.

It's an Italian tradition to include the deceased's photograph on their grave marker; Antonio's is no exception. His plot photo is a formal portrait that captures the quiet dignity of the modest Italian immigrant who did the best he could for both of his families in the most trying of circumstances.

The inscription on his gravestone reads:

Antonio D'Amico

Who lived industriously in the United States of America

wanted to spend his deserved rest in his native land

1891-1964

Everyone in Quadri has a nickname to avoid confusion with generations of cousins who bear the same names. The nickname that Antonio had before he emigrated to the United States has been lost. Upon his return to Italy, the Quadresi referred to him simply as "The American."

To Margherita, he will always be "Papa."

Epilogue

Genealogy may seem like a daunting task. In some instances, it can be…but it doesn't have to be. This is a beginner's guide to basic genealogy. It includes tips to get you started and ways to keep yourself organized and on track. A list of useful links appears at the end of this chapter, including some for video tutorials. The links can also be found in the members' section of BeginningonBoundary.com, which will save you the effort of typing them in. This special website area also includes blank genealogy forms and other charts. The site will be updated whenever possible, so be sure to check in occasionally and see what's been added. The login is (case-sensitive):

Password: BeginoB2018*

Keep in mind that you may never find answers to some of the questions that you have about your family history, but that's OK. You may have other discoveries that outweigh – or at least mitigate – the unknowns. Best wishes on your journey.

Getting started

"Where do I start?" That may be the easiest genealogical question we ever ask. Begin with yourself and work your way back; go from the known to the unknown. Also, decide how far back you'd like to go. For some, it's easier to start with small, manageable goals. Perhaps you're intrigued by a grandparent or an aunt who had passed away before you were born. Make a list of what you know about them and another list of what you don't know about them. Work toward discovering that information.

Designate yourself as the "home" person and build your tree (see the sample chart at the end of this chapter; a chart is also available as a free download at the *Beginning on Boundary* website). Add your parents, grandparents, and so on, going as far back as you possibly can. If you have information about aunts, uncles, siblings, etc., be sure to add them to your tree, too. Not all genealogical mysteries are solved through direct lines back to your 4x grandfather. You must create branches to sort out cousins and other family connections.

If you have a puzzle on your hands within those first few generations, don't be discouraged! Old family bibles, letters, and documents can provide a wealth of information, so be sure to ask family members if those are available for you to examine or photocopy. Also, talk to them and ask concise questions about your family's history: names, birthdates, residences, professions, etc. Write down or record your discussions. If that isn't a fruitful or desired approach, there are plenty of online resources that you can use. Ancestry.com is the most well-known genealogical website. While some may find Ancestry's fees restrictive, keep in mind that a basic membership is twenty dollars per month. You can join for a month or two to try to find the info you want or need, download it, and then deactivate your account. If you need to find more information, you can always reactivate your membership for another month or two. Ancestry is the biggest player by far. The files there are indexed and searchable – and there are billions of them.

FamilySearch.org is a free site (you must create an account) that is owned and operated by the Church of Latter Day Saints, commonly referred to as the Mormon Church. It includes many of the same databases that require a paid account at Ancestry. The main catch is that it isn't always as user-friendly or as easily searchable as Ancestry, and your tree at FamilySearch will be available to other users. Your tree at Ancestry can remain private, if you choose.

If you don't want your family tree online at all, software such as Family Tree Maker will do the trick.

Whatever you do, don't trust your memory and forego recording your connections. Ancestral lines can be overwhelming and confusing.

For example, most Italians utilized a naming convention and tended to follow it rather strictly: The firstborn son was named after the paternal grandfather; the second son was named after the maternal grandfather. Then, the firstborn granddaughter was named after the paternal grandmother, and the second daughter was named for the maternal grandmother. After that, children would be named after other family members, close friends, godparents...or they were simply given a name for no other reason than the parents liked it. While tracing my mother's line, I found that of twelve people born in her small comune in a single year, four had the same name. Fortunately, I found information through a marriage license and death certificate that listed her ancestor's wife and parents, and that helped me track down the correct person out of the four I'd discovered.

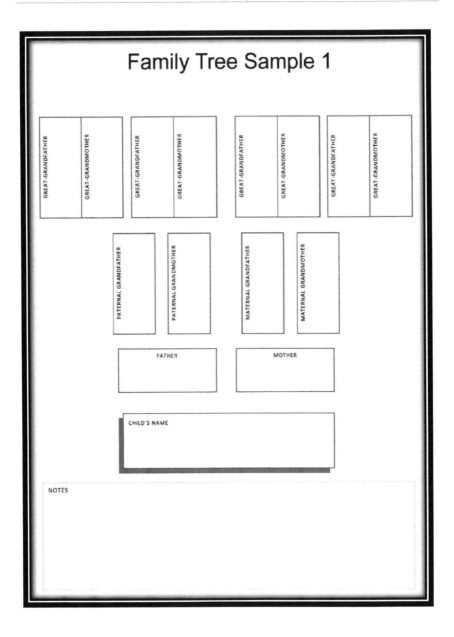

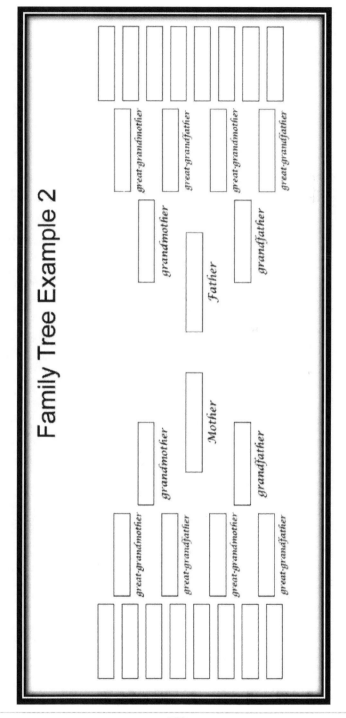

Family Tree Example 2

Documentation is key

There is a popular saying in genealogical circles: "Genealogy without documentation is myth." While oral family history is wonderful and necessary, try to document as much as you can so that you can verify what you've been told. Why is this important? Because sometimes family lore is incorrect. Also, you don't want to waste valuable research time on the wrong family or share incorrect information with others and waste their time, too. Most genealogical websites let you "attach" documentation to each person profiled on your tree, making it easy to organize and reference. If you've decided that you're not going to create an online tree, create file folders for each person in your tree and print out documentation for them. If you're computer savvy, you can do this digitally. Be sure to back up your digital files on a regular basis. Genealogical software will also facilitate this task.

Keep in mind that not all documentation will be found online. While there are billions of digitized records to utilize, there are times when you will need to either write a letter (to get a copy of a birth certificate, for example) or do some legwork (checking dates on gravestones, reading old newspapers on microfilm at the library). While this may not be practical for some, for others it's a piece of cake. If you need assistance, Facebook is chockful of genealogical groups with members who happily want to help. The groups range from basic to advanced, social to serious. There are groups specific not only to ethnicities and family names but nations, cities, and small towns across the world. Simply search Facebook for your surname and the word "genealogy." If you decide to join a Facebook group, don't jump right in and start asking questions. Keep in mind that everyone who joins is anxious to find their roots. Introduce yourself, then observe for a while to better understand the group's purpose and dynamics. The most important thing of all: be polite! Users are eager to help, but rudeness isn't tolerated. I've gotten to know many wonderful people who share the same genealogical interests, and they've shown me ways to quickly search indexed information, have translated Italian for me, and have provided email and snail mail addresses to request information directly from Italy. I would have been lost on my own, spending countless hours researching how to properly do these things. Social media crowdsourcing is invaluable. Don't be afraid to use it. If you can't find a group specific to the name or town you're looking for, consider starting your own. You never know who might turn up.

Using documentation

It's one thing to confirm when an ancestor or relative was born; it may be more of a challenge to sort out their parents' or grandparents' vital information to push your pursuit along. Here are a few tips:

- Some birth and many marriage and death records can be found online through Ancestry or FamilySearch, so do your due diligence there first. Learn how to search the sites and find whatever information you can. Some information may only be obtainable through official channels, though, and availability will vary from state to state. If you're a direct descendant (or the person you're researching was born, married, or died generations ago), you stand a good chance of obtaining records. You may need to provide proof of your connection beforehand, so your own birth certificate (and perhaps your parents') may be necessary. Many records can be ordered online for a fee. If you're intent on learning your family's history, it may be your only course. Typically, birth and marriage records include the names of the parents of the bride and groom. Death records may include the names of the deceased's parents.

- Two search problems face genealogists: common names and unusual names. That covers all the bases, right? Common surnames can be difficult to trace, so look for an unusual first name to use in your search. For example, you may want to know more about Jane Doe who was born in Ohio, but when you search for her, hundreds of possibilities are returned. However, your prior research revealed that Jane Doe's brothers were named Josiah and Jasper. While those names aren't all that unusual, searching for Jane *with* Josiah and Jasper could lead to more information. You might pull up a census record, yearbook, or some other material to grow your tree and lead you to more info. With unusual surnames, try misspelling the name and/or Anglicizing it for your inquiries. For example, my grandfather, Giuseppe D'Arcangelo, was also known as Giuseppe Angelo, Guiseppe Angelo (misspelled first name), Joseph Angelo, Joe Angelo…the list goes on.

- Depending on the year, the U.S. census can be a treasure trove of information. I discovered my Aunt Sara by doing some math from information that was collected specifically for the 1930 census. Citizens were asked to provide their age at the time of their first marriage. My grandparents' marriage was easily and correctly calculated, but my grandmother's second marriage, to Antonio, was not. We believed that Antonio's marriage to my grandmother was his first, but that notion was quickly disproved when I took a harder look at that census record. Without careful study and a bit of detective work, it would have been easy to overlook that life-altering bit of information that brought our wonderful Aunt Sara and her family into our lives. Review census information and glean as much from it as you possibly can – and be sure to give it some thought while looking for the big picture. Actually, that last bit of advice is true for all documents you find.

- Immigration records can hold a wealth of information, but keep in mind that not everyone arrived in the United States through Ellis Island. Some entered through New Orleans, Philadelphia, Boston, Canada, Mexico, San Francisco…practically any port city. The best way to search immigration records is through Ancestry. FamilySearch links their immigration records to EllisIsland.org. The account is free, but they charge a fee to send you the records (thirty dollars per record at the time of this writing). Ancestry includes this in your membership. Their records not only include ship manifests but, in many cases, photos of the ships themselves. You may download all the records and photos to your computer, and most are suitable for photographic printing.

Giuseppe's entry in the St. Albans list for Canadian border crossings into the United States. Note the misspelling of his first name. What information can you glean from this card that might be useful? We see that his wife's name was Rosa and she resided in Quadri. Note that his destination is Canonsburg, PA.

DNA

Continuing advancements in DNA testing have added an additional layer of intrigue to genealogical research and have created a new field known as *genetic genealogy*. For example, if you're adopted and interested in knowing more about your ethnicity, DNA testing will give you some answers – but it can do much more than that. Adoptees and birth parents are now using it to discover their birth families, with varying degrees of success.

DNA testing can also reveal a Non-Parental Event, commonly known as an NPE. Sometimes testers discover that they are not the biological child of their mother or father, or that they are – or have – a half-sibling. As you can imagine, reactions to this sort of news differ widely, with some NPE being joyfully accepted by their birth families, while others face rejection. If you decide to DNA test, be aware that the results may have consequences not only for yourself but others, too, including people you may not know.

For my mom, DNA testing solved one lifelong mystery but also revealed some disturbing news. In the end, she received some answers and a better understanding of her childhood situation, so it was well worth it to her. However, you may want to carefully weigh the pros and cons of DNA testing before proceeding.

There are several companies that do DNA testing, with Ancestry having the largest database. The website GEDMatch.com allows users to upload their results from Ancestry, FamilyTree, and other services. In some instances, the pool is broader at GEDMatch because it includes people who've not tested on Ancestry, or they're from other nations. It also provides more detailed results. The basic membership is free, and I recommend it.

Resources

Keep in mind that a paid membership to Ancestry may include information from several of these sources. For example, an All-Access membership includes full access to premium sites like Newspapers.com, the military records site Fold3.com, and international records. You may circumvent some of these paid sites by using FamilySearch for international records or by using Google's Newspaper Archive instead of Newspapers.com. These searches may be a little more challenging, but if you have the time and patience, you can save a few dollars. Also, try Googling your ancestors; you may find some details that you didn't know, leading to newspaper articles or someone else's family tree that contains the information you need.

- **Genealogy sites**
  Ancestry.com ($)
  FamilySearch.org
  Genealogy.com ($)
  MyHeritage.com ($)
- **Newspapers**
  Newspapers.com ($)
  News.Google.com/newspapers
- **Graves**
  FindAGrave.com
  BillionGraves.com
- **Military records**
  Ancestry.com ($)
  Archives.com ($)
  Fold3.com ($)
- **General**
  USGenWeb.org
  Archives.gov/research/genealogy
  Archives.com (Free/$)

- **How-to**

  YouTube.com/user/AncestryCom

  FamilySearch.org/ask/learningViewer/733

- **DNA Testing**

  Note that you must pay for your initial DNA test, but the sites marked with an asterisk allow you to upload your results from Ancestry to broaden your DNA search.

  Ancestry.com

  GedMatch.com *

  FamilyTreeDNA.com *

  23andMe.com

Notes

All photographs by Rosemary Capanna or from the Capanna Family Collection, except where noted.

Cover photo: Boundary Street, November 12, 1926. Pittsburgh City Photographer Collection, 1901-2002, AIS.1971.05, Archives Service Center, University of Pittsburgh.

BeginningonBoundary.com

More photos may be found on the website.

The D'Arcangelo, D'Aloisio, and D'Amico family trees may be found on the website.

1. Choate, Mark. 2008. Emigrant Nation: The making of Italy abroad. Cambridge, MA: Harvard University Press.

2. Luciano J. Iorizzo, Italian immigration and the impact of the padrone system (1980) p. 160.

3. American Psychiatric Association. (2013) Diagnostic and statistical manual of mental disorders, (5th ed.). Washington, DC: Author.
https://www.ptsd.va.gov/professional/PTSD-overview/dsm5_criteria_ptsd.asp

DSM-5 Criteria for PTSD

(1). All of the criteria are required for the diagnosis of PTSD.

The following text summarizes the diagnostic criteria:

Criterion A (one required): The person was exposed to: death, threatened death, actual or threatened serious injury, or actual or threatened sexual violence, in the following way(s): Direct exposure

- Witnessing the trauma
- Learning that a relative or close friend was exposed to a trauma
- Indirect exposure to aversive details of the trauma, usually in the course of professional duties (e.g., first responders, medics)

Criterion B (one required): The traumatic event is persistently re-experienced, in the following way(s):

- Intrusive thoughts
- Nightmares
- Flashbacks
- Emotional distress after exposure to traumatic reminders
- Physical reactivity after exposure to traumatic reminders

Criterion C (one required): Avoidance of trauma-related stimuli after the trauma, in the following way(s):

- Trauma-related thoughts or feelings
- Trauma-related reminders

Criterion D (two required): Negative thoughts or feelings that began or worsened after the trauma, in the following way(s):

- Inability to recall key features of the trauma
- Overly negative thoughts and assumptions about oneself or the world
- Exaggerated blame of self or others for causing the trauma

- Negative affect
- Decreased interest in activities
- Feeling isolated
- Difficulty experiencing positive affect

Criterion E (two required): Trauma-related arousal and reactivity that began or worsened after the trauma, in the following way(s):

- Irritability or aggression
- Risky or destructive behavior
- Hypervigilance
- Heightened startle reaction
- Difficulty concentrating
- Difficulty sleeping

Criterion F (required): Symptoms last for more than 1 month.

Criterion G (required): Symptoms create distress or functional impairment (e.g., social, occupational).

Criterion H (required): Symptoms are not due to medication, substance use, or other illness.

Two specifications:

Dissociative Specification. In addition to meeting criteria for diagnosis, an individual experiences high levels of either of the following in reaction to trauma-related stimuli:

Depersonalization. experience of being an outside observer of or detached from oneself (e.g., feeling as if "this is not happening to me" or one were in a dream).

Derealization: experience of unreality, distance, or distortion (e.g., "things are not real").

Delayed Specification. Full diagnostic criteria are not met until at least six months after the trauma(s), although onset of symptoms may occur immediately.

Kickstarter Thank Yous

Beginning on Boundary was made possible through a Kickstarter crowdfunding campaign. My warmest thanks to the following for their support.

James Abel

Susan Anderson

Paula Antonelli

Mark & Carolyn Arends

Ron Barry

Ken Berczik

The Bernadowski-Knapp Family

D'Shan Berry

Erma Bonadero

Broooose Brown

Marielle, Noah, and Lily Brown

The Buday Family

Pamela & Dennis Chiedor

Renita Cipriani

Richard Colelli

James Corrie

Ed Crabtree & Tim O'Hara

Sharon Dixon

Mark R. Dopita

Donna & Dave Draeger

M.K. Driscoll

Cori Garlock

Gene & Carol

Chris Gennaula

Paula Gutosky

Rand Iserman

Bill Jacobsen

JimmyC

Joy Jonat

Laura Koepnick

Dia Kulak

Lisa Laschen-Zilka

Lori McCann

Brianne Mitchell

Dr. Jeanne Natali

Donna Nicholson

Janine Maloney

Clare Mucho

Melissa O'Brien

Justine Olawsky

Marilyn Pankratz

Kristin Pearson

Joe and Claudette Pellasce

Pamela Powell-Duricic

Patty Revak

Denise Whitehead Roadman

Diane Tallerico Robb

Judy Rodman

The Rogers Family

Rob Sargent

Sharon R.

Bernie "Queen Berniqua" Sheahan

Jean M. Smith

LA Smith-Buxton

Gail Stobaugh

Virginia Stringer

Lynn Tautkus

Nora Thornton

Phil Troop

Margaret Vitalis

Tricia Walker

Darlene Beatty Walters

Gina Walters

Woody

70730718R00104

Made in the USA
Middletown, DE
16 April 2018